The Prosperous Hotelier: A Guide to Hotel Financial Literacy for the Hospitality Professional

Most hoteliers operate under the philosophy, "Look after the guests and the money looks after itself." The truth is the money never looks after itself—you need to be and stay on top of it every day in this industry we call hospitality. David spells out clear and executable strategies that any hotel leader can use to be more financially effective and a better leader.

~ **Chip Conley,** Founder, Modern Elder Academy, *New York Times* bestselling author, Former CEO and founder of Joie de Vivre Hospitality, Former Head of Hospitality and Strategy at Airbnb

As someone who writes about the hospitality industry for a living, I find David Lund's financial perspective is invaluable in my ability to understand the nuances of hotel finance—clearly and concisely. David possesses the exceptional ability to write about complicated subject matter and convey it in a way that is simple and succinct to understand—for the tyro starting out or for the expert who needs a refresher.

   The Prosperous Hotelier should be on the desk of every hotel GM and accessible to anyone interested in the financial success of a hotel asset, which, when it comes down to it, is every employee. His writing breaks down esoteric financial concepts in a way that is easily digestible and, in the long run, will help a hotel, a hotel portfolio or a hotel company bolster their bottom lines.

~ **David Eisen,** VP, Editor-In Chief, *HOTELS Magazine*

A thoughtful and well-articulated guide for hoteliers at all levels of seniority and experience. David has an incredible ability to simplify and teach an area of the business that is often misunderstood and even feared.

~ **Michael Grove,** Chief Operating Officer, HOTSTATS

There is a general misconception that understanding the financials of a hotel is best left to professionals with formal education in accounting, as these financials are perceived to be too complex and challenging for those without such a background. However, David Lund's new book *The Prosperous*

Hotelier debunks this myth and will help you demystify the financials of the hotel industry. Whether you're a seasoned hotelier or just in the early stages of your hospitality career, this book will provide valuable insights and inspiration. I highly endorse this book and give it my highest recommendation.

~ **Henri Roelings,** Publisher, hospitalitynet.org

The Prosperous Hotelier is the best guide for success in the hotel business I have ever read. In an easy-to-read style, David simplifies the complexities of hotel finances for operational leaders. Regardless of your department or position, if you are a leader in a hotel, you need to be a *financial* leader. This book shows you how with common sense and practical examples. Pay attention!

~ **David Garcelon,** Hotel Manager, Fairmont Hotels

This book is for you if you want the most comprehensive collection of financial leadership strategies. David provides the most straightforward method for financial leadership, regardless of whether you are a seasoned hotelier or an aspiring hospitality leader. I had the opportunity to work with David on several occasions in both his team workshops and mentoring program, and I saw firsthand the advantages of his straightforward approach to financial leadership.

~ **Patrick McClary,** CEO/Founder, CORE Food & Beverage Consulting

I highly endorse *The Prosperous Hotelier* by David Lund. As someone who has participated in several financial leadership training courses led by David, I can attest to David's expertise and ability to convey complex financial concepts in an easy-to-understand manner. This book provides valuable insights and practical strategies for financial success in the hospitality industry, and I highly recommend it to anyone looking to enhance their financial leadership skills.

~ **Claude Brock,** CFO, KSL Resorts

The switch that brings light to your hotel finance understanding, making it easy and clear for everyone—for financial and non-financial people. With clear and easy explanations, David shows you that what you need to get is a sense of business through a good understanding of your reports, forecasts, etc., and the way your property works. This book will become a bible for the hotel business . . . for sure.

~ **Olivier Lot,** Resort Manager

This is a must-read for hotel professionals. I had the pleasure of working with David in San Francisco and can confidently say that he is a true expert in hotel accounting and finance. His new book is a comprehensive guide offering valuable insights and practical advice for hotel professionals looking to improve their financial management skills.

From budgeting and forecasting to cost control and reporting, this book covers all the essential topics that are crucial to the success of any hotel operation. David has brought his years of experience in hospitality and deep understanding of the financial side of the business to create a must-read for anyone looking to stay ahead of the curve in this highly competitive industry.

I highly recommend *The Prosperous Hotelier* to any hotel professional looking to take their financial management skills to the next level.

~ **Adam Knight,** Co-Founder and CEO, Recreation Vacation Rentals

David Lund has spent his career elevating leaders by growing their business acumen. In this well-structured book, David draws upon years of experience as a trusted coach to make financial leadership approachable. First-time managers and experienced hoteliers alike are sure to benefit from his clearly deliberate and thoughtful presentation of concepts, ideas and best practices that help leaders strike the balance between hospitality-smart and business-smart. A must-read for any hospitality professional looking for a competitive advantage.

~ **Tim Ostrem,** MBA, Area Director, Atlific Hotels

For anyone looking to build on their financial acumen, find their financial "superpowers," and deepen their understanding of hotel operations, this is the book for you. Through his relatable stories, David Lund outlines the steps to take to have the right financial leadership skills for a prosperous career and a prosperous life.

~ **Jamie Caraher,** President & CEO at Lodging Dynamics

I highly recommend *The Prosperous Hotelier* to any hotel pro who wants to maximize their potential in the hotel industry. Actually, many of the principles apply to any business, and actually they apply to your personal finance as well! I love how David weaves in the concept of mindset throughout all of his teaching. What paralyzes most people from mastering their hotel's finances is believing that they aren't a numbers person or that the numbers are somehow too complex for them. This is not true! Understanding the basics of hotel financial statements is going to help anyone add more value to their organization and go further faster. *The Prosperous Hotelier* will help you master those basics and then take you as deep as you want to go. You just have to decide you can, and get started!

~ **Katie Paolino,** Partner Hotel Solutions

The Prosperous Hotelier is a must-read for hoteliers at all stages in their career. Coach David brings a hands-on approach that is relevant and fun for everyone and really helps engage hoteliers in areas that they may not engage in in their normal day to day. Great read! My team will be getting copies!

~ **Ray Roberge,** General Manager, Delta Hotels by Marriott Beausejour

David's book is what operations managers have been missing. The lessons he includes and the practical explanations remove the confusion and fear around the numbers, allowing leaders to confidently take the next steps in their career. I recommend it to anyone who wants to prosper in this business we call hospitality.

~ **Saurabh Mehta,** General Manager, 1 King West, Toronto

The Prosperous Hotelier is a life-changing tool for operational leaders to truly look at the business through an entrepreneurial lens. Nowhere else can you find such a candid instrument to understand the numbers and how they relate to the daily routine of a busy hotel. David makes this learning process easy and fun. And surprisingly, you end up loving finances no matter what your role is in the organization. This is a book to keep on your night table at all times.

~ **Gamal El Fakih Rodriguez,** Vice President of Operations (Luxury), Caribbean and Latin America, Marriott International

From David's lectern to your library, Lund's essential financial wisdom is now at our fingertips. Never on a shelf, *The Prosperous Hotelier* must be on the corner of your desk, beaten, dog-eared, coffee-stained with passages underlined and excerpts read aloud. There is nothing passive about our industry, and this book emphasises repeatedly that if we are going to be successful in this business, we must engage the lessons of this book and very actively implement them into our daily hotel lives.

~ **Jim Bence,** President/CEO Hospitality Saskatchewan

The Prosperous Hotelier shows us that the numbers are not the hard part of hospitality. It shows that if one approaches the business of hotels with attention and passion, the mystery of the financial piece evaporates. Creating superior results around the numbers is not only possible, it's what will happen.

~ **Brett Hollenbeck,** Associate Professor of Marketing at the UCLA Anderson School of Management.

The Prosperous Hotelier isn't just a finance book—it takes you on a journey through David's career while explaining hospitality financials in a relatable way.

For hospitality leaders, financial management can be daunting and often overlooked. David not only explains financial leadership but provides real examples that can be taken back to your business. In order to generate an ROI for investors, it's crucial that all levels of management possess a strong understanding of financial leadership and the ability to share that knowledge. *The Prosperous Hotelier* shows us how to do that!

~ **Ryan Cochrane,** Corporate Director of Operations, MasterBUILT Hotels

After more than twenty-five years covering hospitality, I finally understand how property-level financials work! Thank you, David, for demystifying what seemed overwhelming and complicated, and for turning it into something fun and easy to learn.

~ **Glenn Haussman,** #1 Hospitality Podcast (No Vacancy), Event Speaker, Board Member at LI Hospitality Association & Creative Xchange

David's ability to explain, to make it real, and to educate on the simple principles of hotel finance is remarkable. His human approach explaining the reality of financial hotel management for junior, middle and executive management is a tool that everyone can benefit from. A must read. (And keep it on the desk. You will use it again and again.)

~ **Ingrid Jarrett,** President & CEO, British Columbia Hotel Association

To all hotel salespeople: Get the book, read the book, and keep the book as a reference. David's book takes the fear out of that upcoming owner's or P/L meeting. Trust me.

~ **Andrea E. Gonzalez,** CMP, DES, CHBA, Founder and CEO, RESET Marketing and Events

Through *The Prosperous Hotelier*, David has set in print what he has done so well teaching in-person—he makes financial acumen relatable, approachable and, surprisingly, interesting! He makes space at the financial "table" for all leaders, with the belief that everyone, at all organizational levels, must contribute for shared success. Knowledge is power, and for "operational" leaders David's approach is both convincing and heartfelt. His desire to see them prosper as leaders, and in life, is as strong as his desire to see the same for the hotels they lead.

~ **Ken Flores,** General Manager, Fairmont Hotels

The Prosperous Hotelier is a great place to find all of David's hospitality financial tips and advice in one place. This book can appeal to both financial and non-financial-minded individuals in the hospitality industry and is a great resource to have on hand. I know my copy will be within reaching distance at all times while I am at work!

~ **Megan Wood,** CPA, Vice President of Accounting and Finance – Oxford Group

A comprehensive guide on how effective financial management and business practices can contribute to the balanced scorecard in any hotel. The format provides an effective blueprint for new managers taking on P&L responsibility or experienced leaders requiring more in-depth skills to engage with senior leadership and owners to maximize performance.

~ **Chris Cahill,** Former Deputy CEO Accor, EVP Las Vegas Sands, & President/COO Fairmont Hotels

In this book, hospitality maverick David Lund provides a simple and practical approach to decoding finance and teaches us how to transform that understanding into actionable leadership skills. As someone who has worked in the hospitality industry for many years, I have found this book invaluable.

It offers practical strategies and insights that can help anyone in a leadership role better understand and manage financial performance and ultimately drive success in their organization.

What I appreciate most about *The Prosperous Hotelier* is how it presents complex financial concepts in a way that is easy to understand and apply. David Lund's writing style is engaging and straightforward, making it accessible to readers of all levels of financial literacy.

I believe *The Prosperous Hotelier* is a must-read for anyone in the hospitality industry who wants to improve their leadership skills and drive tremendous financial success.

~ **Michael Tingsager,** Founder, Hospitality Mavericks

David gives our industry an approachable and practical how-to guide for financial success. Implementing these principles and processes created a culture of ownership with our management and better results for our business. I know this book will become an important tool for the training and development of our managers.

~ **Brooke Christianson,** Owner, Canalta Hotels

I was so incredibly fortunate to have had these insights and principles taught to me by David early in my career as a Chef. They gave me confidence and built a foundation for me to become a Subject Matter Expert in Hotel F&B finances and controls. This book instills the principle that everyone has a role in the financial health of the business every day, not just the last day of the month. I have passed along these learnings to so many of my leaders who have worked with me through the years. They continually share with me how this has helped them get promoted into their current roles at their hotels no matter the brand, the hotel, or the country they are in.

David's approach to removing the fear and providing the knowledge to all levels of leadership has created generations of great hoteliers who are successfully employing the learnings that he has proven work. After all, great processes and controls in F&B finances allow you to be focused on the opportunities rather than fighting P&L fires every month.

No matter where you are in your Hospitality Career, whether you are in your first role or the Hotel GM and beyond, you will have personal and professional success with these teachings. I encourage you to keep this book close—the insightful and easy understanding offered by the QR Codes are a great way to keep you and your teams engaged and on the same page.

And Chefs: Are you committed or just involved? As you know, taste is truly subjective but the technique is not. It is either right or wrong. This book and its teachings may be more important to your future successes than your entire collection of cook books. What you learn here should be passed along with diligence and purpose as if teaching a new cook how to make an omelet. The foundation will stick with them forever.

~ **Chad Blunston,** Corporate Director of Culinary Training, White Lodging

The smartest people make complex subjects simple and intuitive. That is exactly what David has done with this book. Business acumen is essential for any leader, but accounting and finance can be intimidating, and some leaders make it that way intentionally. David does an outstanding job distilling key financial concepts and practices leaders need to know to run a successful hotel. This book is easy to read, and it will benefit both experienced leaders and young professionals starting their career.

~ **Ian Wilson,** CEO Wilson Innovation Lab, ex SVP Non-Gaming Operations, Marina Bay Sands

I believe every hotelier should have this book—EVERY ONE OF THEM! Compartmentalizing departments and not allowing them to participate in the financial pillar of the hotel is clearly not working. This book is easy to follow, the videos are instructive, and everyone who uses it can become a hotel finance person. I always talk about adding tools to our "toolbox," and this book is one of the best tools we can add. It should be shared with all staff. We often talk about how everything in the hotel costs money, and this book will help staff understand this and learn to care for the financial health of the property.

~ **Lisa Martin**, Regional Controller, Davidson Hospitality

THE
PROSPEROUS
HOTELIER

THE
PROSPEROUS
HOTELIER

A Guide to Hotel Financial Literacy
for the Hospitality Professional

DAVID LUND

MAURICE BASSETT

The Prosperous Hotelier: A Guide to Hotel Financial Literacy for the Hospitality Professional (*The Prosperous Series #3*)

Maurice Bassett
P.O. Box 839
Anna Maria, FL 34216

Contact the publisher:
MauriceBassett@gmail.com

Contact the author:
david@hotelfinancialcoach.com

Editing and interior layout: Chris Nelson
Cover design and illustrations: David Michael Moore

ISBN: 978-1-60025-165-8

Library of Congress Control Number: 2023936123

First Edition

Dedication

I proudly dedicate this book to my father, Mervyn. My dad was a community college teacher. To say the least I was not a great student, but he never gave up on me. He would say, "David, you can do anything with your life so long as you're willing to work for it."

He was right.

TABLE OF CONTENTS

I. FINANCIAL LEADERSHIP | 1

II. BUSINESS PRINCIPLES AND FINANCIAL STATEMENTS | 55

III. MANAGING PAYROLL AND EXPENSES | 113

IV. COST OF GOODS AND FOOD AND BEVERAGE CONTROLS |141

V. HOTEL BUSINESS STRATEGY AND FINANCIAL ANALYSIS | 171

VI. Effective Leadership with the Numbers | 215

Foreword

Who would have thought that two junior accounting clerks working in Food and Beverage Control (a department that doesn't even exist anymore) would be writing a book—and a Foreword for said book? Yet, here we are, with career paths that intersected through CP Hotels and Fairmont Hotels over the last forty years. David excelled in his lane and developed expertise as a leader in hotel finance and accounting, while I continued to chart my path in Sales and Marketing. Fast forward to 2007 and I had just finished my MBA when I had an opportunity to change career paths from Fairmont's Global Vice President of Sales and Distribution to the dark side, as the Regional Vice President and General Manager. As I have said many times when I talk about my career path, I don't think . . . No, let me correct that, I *know* I would not have been as successful without an incredible team. There are many people I worked with whom I could mention, but the one who was the most impactful and who definitely stands out above the crowd was my Regional Director of Finance, David Lund.

Why? Two reasons. First and foremost, David is highly intelligent, helpful and a very patient person. He is so passionate and knowledgeable about finance and accounting, and the hotel business in general. And two, something I will always admire David for and which is somewhat rare in the hotel business: David has always had a balanced approach to life. He structured his time so he would be at work when he needed to be and not be there when he did not need to be. This seems like such a simple concept, but it's often difficult to manage in hospitality, and it reflects David's deep awareness of the moving parts of the hotel business.

You might think I simply did a quick summary review of *The Prosperous Hotelier* in order to write this Foreword for an old friend and colleague. But you would be incorrect—I read it cover to cover. I kept two viewpoints in mind as I green-highlighted my way through the chapters: that of an experienced leader who has been in the business for a long time, and that of myself, way back at the beginning of my hotel career beginning the journey that had me growing up in this industry.

My first takeaway from *The Prosperous Hotelier* relates to the two prevalent aspects at play through every chapter of the book: David's passion for the potential of a hotel's performance, and his undeniable depth of knowledge and expertise regarding hotel financial leadership. When you consider the depth of interconnectivity related to a hotel's financial workings you see that the whole is more than the sum of its parts. David helps us see this interconnectedness. This is demonstrated by the comprehensive nature of the book, which moves well beyond the areas traditionally covered by a Director of Finance to scope out what every leader in a hotel should hold themselves accountable to regarding financial and accounting matters. David and I agree that to truly succeed in the hospitality business you need to not only understand the financial fundamentals but—and even more importantly—to understand and apply financial leadership. Both of these themes are palpable through the entire book and it makes you want to read more; he pulls you into the realm of financial leadership—which, by the way, is saying a lot given that it is usually a fairly dry topic.

My second takeaway from this book is around the perspective of new leaders. There is no doubt in my mind that it would have been a significant advantage to have read this book when I was starting out.

There are so many pearls of wisdom, so many detailed explanations on procedures and concepts, and so many questions answered that you would either not know to ask or be afraid to ask. And it isn't a boring textbook! It is all written in an easy to comprehend manner.

Usually during training your direct boss or peer walks you through your various job tasks: forecasting, scheduling, RPI, and so on. This book will fast-track your training by augmenting it with the explanations as to why each element of the training is important and how it fits together within the structure of the hotel. It reminds me of our days at The Fairmont Royal York when David held training sessions for the new leaders. There was typically a turning point, a moment of comprehension, when you saw that these new leaders *understood the why behind their everyday tasks.* For every new supervisor (and some experienced department heads) *The Prosperous Hotelier* will be the hotel bible on financial leadership. It will help anyone in the hotel industry better understand all of the pieces that make up the hotel financial leadership puzzle.

To sum it all up (pun intended), I feel strongly that this book should be read by a majority of leaders in our industry. It is a type of self-help book for new and seasoned leaders alike. This book will provide guidance and broader understanding to all leaders – from the General Manager all the way to the first time supervisor in the hotel bar/restaurant. (Incidentally, in Chapter 46 David talks about the General Managers who he felt did not have the financial acumen needed. For the record, I was one of his many General Managers over the years, whom he rightly calls to the carpet!)

A final thought: one of the often-cited comments from female leaders is that they are not strong in finance. This book is for you, too. It is a chapter-by-chapter, self-guided tour through the landscape of financial leadership. If you are in the hotel business and buy into the philosophy of developing your leaders and sharing information across all levels of the leadership group, then financial leadership is a concept that will build strong teamwork, likely create more time for leaders to focus on the guest—and most certainly drive profit.

Happy reading.

Heather McCrory
Chief Executive Officer, North & Central America, Accor

Introduction

Having worked in the hotel business for over four decades, I know most people think the numbers are the "hard" part of hospitality. There's a common belief that the financials are best left to professionals who can sort out the complex interplay between the different departments of a hotel. It's just too challenging and complicated for anyone who didn't go to accounting school.

This idea is just a myth—one you can bust wide open with this book.

As hotel employees, we all grow up in the world of guest service and colleague engagement. Then one day we find ourselves in a different world. A new place where we are expected to manage our department and the numbers too.

If that's you—welcome to the big leagues. This book is for you.

And if you aspire to the big leagues, well—welcome aboard. This book can help you get there faster and far more prepared and ready for action.

I've worked with hundreds of hotel leaders, so I know that having confidence and knowledge around the financials is the key to a successful hotel career and—to a very large extent—your own personal prosperity. Every successful hotel executive knows that the numbers are the currency for advancement. And their secret is this: it's not accounting but "hotel-business thinking" that you need to cultivate and possess. It's seeing that the component parts of a hotel can be integrated into a seamless whole—and understanding the financials is the key to doing this.

I spent the first ten years of my hotel career in operations. I know what managers and leaders deal with every day. I also know how your typical hotel financial person makes the numbers seem mysterious and confusing. *The Prosperous Hotelier* was written to show in a straightforward way what the numbers mean and how you can bring financial skills and abilities into your world.

This book is about the business of hotels, and it's written for two types of colleagues:

1. Non-financial people who want to cross that bridge and become leaders who possess hospitality business mojo. In these pages I explain the language of the hotel business in clear, relatable examples, using stories from the front lines and the back of the house. I've lived it all.

2. Financial leaders and managers who want to do what I do: bring everyone into the loop around the finances with all aspects of hotel operations, because once everyone's on board, everything runs more smoothly, and everyone's happier. We're all part of something bigger—together.

Along the way I'll share a lot of what I've learned as a financial leader in hospitality, and how I was able to unlock what didn't work for me and my leadership and make it work. How I was able to take my communication and leadership abilities to a whole new level. In sharing these details with you, I hope you'll see yourself in them and cultivate the ability to effectively engage with your colleagues and the numbers.

I have personally helped many individuals just like you overcome their fear and uncertainty around hotel financials. It's my passion.

Don't wait to get started! No one is coming to save you and do the heavy lifting. You have the ability to change your world and create a prosperous life with the hospitality financial leadership skills I'm sharing in this book. Put them to good use, and before you know it, you'll be swinging in the big leagues.

A few notes to help you while reading the book.

1. Most of the book is written from the perspective of a financial leader, Controller or Director of Finance, but not always. Sometimes it comes from an operational leader or General Manager's viewpoint. Sometimes it's slanted to the corporate or regional office view of things. This will help you see why certain concepts and processes are so important.

2. Broadly speaking there are three different business models in the hotel world. The "owner operator," the "franchise" and the "branded/managed." This book is largely slanted to the view of the branded/managed hotel.

3. The hotel business is not a science but rather an expression of ideas and best practices. The book lays out what I think based on my experience having worked inside a global 4-star brand for over thirty years. The hotels I worked in were full-service, with large staffs and leadership teams. Much of what is in this book is based on this experience.

4. I often repeat the main themes and strategies, and I do so on purpose for three reasons. One, it's important stuff and I want you to get it on a DNA level. Secondly, I believe it's how we learn best—by seeing a similar idea more than once. Third, the themes I repeat are pervasive and show up in different places and events throughout the financial and operational landscape of the hotel.

5. There are QR codes throughout the book that will take you to additional resources, including videos and spreadsheets, to enhance your learning and experience.

This book does not claim to be a comprehensive presentation of the inner workings of hotels and their financials. I doubt any book could do this, especially because the hospitality industry is changing all the time and there's never a shortage of different opinions! But it's based on my more than forty years in hotels, holding various positions, including entry-level ones like bartender, waiter, front desk clerk, room and food and beverage operations, and so on. I moved on to a position in food and beverage control, and quite by accident ended up in an accounting role. My operational experience provided me with a unique outlook as my responsibilities in accounting grew, later, as a Controller and Hotel Manager, Corporate Director of Financial Systems and Analysis. My earlier positions influenced how I did those later jobs, and gave me a unique, more holistic perspective on hotel financial operations. I have been a coach and consultant for the industry for the past ten years.

I hope that what I share here at the very least helps deepen your understanding of hotel operations and supports you in your career growth and satisfaction. Onward!

I

FINANCIAL LEADERSHIP

This section lays out the concept of what financial leadership is all about for the reader, their career, and their prosperity.

Chapter 1

How It All Began

My primary responsibility as the head of the finance and accounting departments in the hotel was to ensure the books were clean and balanced. What I really got paid for was serving as the "chief financial information officer." The reality was that much of the time, the financial information I had to work with stunk!

In every business, communication is important. But around the financial piece of the business, communication is key. Great communication can make the business successful, help it grow, cause it to take on a life of its own. Poor communication can make the business die either a long, lingering death or a swift, unexpected one. But death is death. Death is painful, even in business. It means the death of that business owner's and/or the investors' hopes and dreams.

Good communication in business is, therefore, a matter of survival.

Hotels follow the same pattern, especially regarding communication about the money coming in and going out. No communication on the financial numbers translates into poor results without understanding why. For instance: incomplete financial statements with the telltale signs of missing invoices and bungled accruals, and budgets and forecasts that totally miss the mark—all of which feeds financial failure. Put all that on top of monthly financial commentaries that don't make any sense because supporting documents don't exist.

This was what I was producing back then.

I knew what was needed in order to do my job properly, but I couldn't get the 75-plus other non-financial leaders in the hotel to help me.

As the financial leader, I knew I couldn't just sit in my office and dream up what was going to happen next month in the kitchen, the laundry, the dining room or any other area of the hotel with any accuracy. The hotel business does not work that way. To be successful, the financial information must come from the department heads, because they are the experts in their departments. But also, each of these experts must take ownership of the information and goals set. And in turn, each one takes ownership of the desired results.

I tried everything I knew to get these managers to play ball with me. I wrote tons of memos, preached hundreds of sermons at department head meetings, and cornered countless managers for one-to-one discussions where I only stopped short of dropping to my knees to beg. All of it was to no avail. What I wanted or needed didn't matter to them. They had their own worries, wants and needs.

The reports I received in exchange for my heartache were either incomplete, not accurate, late or nowhere to be seen. It felt awful to work so hard, with such passion, and still fail, still produce lousy work. I was pretty sure this gig was not going to last too long because it was moving in this downward, unproductive direction. I ended every day feeling frustrated and alone.

~

The new general manager came to my office one day and asked what was going on in the financial area. I discussed the frustration I had with the other managers and their lack of follow-through in providing the financial information I needed to produce good results.

I wanted him to say something like: "Leave it to me. I'll light a fire under them!" But he didn't.

Instead, he said something unimaginable. "Why don't you create a workshop for the managers? Call it 'Hotel Finances for Dummies' or something like that."

I paused for a split second, let my mouth and emotions overrun my brain, and blurted out, "I don't have time. Look at my desk. I'm already here ten or more hours a day trying to do this job. And I'm not a teacher."

His calm reply was, "You can do this! And, David, it's the right thing to do."

As he stood to leave, his parting comment was, "As an incentive to inspire you, this little workshop is now part of your annual bonus criteria. No workshop, no bonus, Mr. Lund."

Somewhat reluctantly, but with this new carrot being held out in front of me, I set about putting this monster training together.

Where to start? What information to include? Where to get the information? How to ask for what I needed in a different way than what had already not worked?

Days and weeks passed as I worked to address the questions in my own mind about the who, what, where when and how of this presentation. Given my previous lack of success and having tried all methods of persuasion I could think of already, I didn't feel very confident about the workshop results. After all, it's accounting!

The workshop day arrived. Human resources handpicked thirty-five of the hotel's leaders to attend my first-ever financial workshop from 9:30 a.m. until 4:30 p.m. Six hours of teaching time. I was scared. I dreaded the idea of standing in front of thirty-five hotel managers (who typically ran or hid when they saw me headed toward them) and talking about accounting all day.

"Yea! Everybody loves accounting! Not!" I told myself.

Then a little voice whispered back, "That's the whole point of doing this workshop. Try to teach each of them the value in the numbers and the value they have in the process."

"That's an impossible task," I thought at 9:15 a.m. as everyone dragged themselves to a seat.

But as the day progressed, I gained more and more confidence, and ultimately something magical happened. It wasn't all perfect by any means. I think some of my examples were hard for the attendees to follow, and a few of the hands-on exercises were received with only minimal enthusiasm. But overall, the day went much better than expected. As it turned out, I was the harshest critic in the room.

But it was what happened at the end of the afternoon that blew my mind and redirected my thinking.

I wrapped things up and unexpectedly got a small round of applause. I then handed out a short evaluation form with ten questions, asking participants to rate the workshop from 1 to 5. Then I excused everyone and sent them on their way.

A couple of the department leaders stopped and took their time to thank me. Before I knew it, I had a small line of managers waiting to thank me.

Me!

After only six hours of teaching time, I got some amazing compliments that shook me to the core. I had taught them to value their roles in the financial piece of the pie and to value each other, and in that I felt valued, too.

I knew right then and there how wrong I'd been to think this training would be a waste of time. It had turned out to be something BIG. And for my part, it was an amazing feeling to motivate, inspire and train these leaders in a profound way.

The responses I got from the surveys revealed some incredible comments. Here are a few:

"Finally, someone explained the P&L."

"We should all have had this training from day one."

"I had no idea what you did with my forecast."

"I didn't know my financial forecast input mattered."

"The owners actually see my projections."

"Owners actually care about my projections."

"Sorry! I thought I was just doing your job for you. I didn't understand until today that what you asked for really made my job easier."

In the coming weeks, I was asked to host a second workshop. It filled up quickly as word spread about the first one's success. We even started a waiting list.

Early the following year, the hotel I worked for submitted the workshop concept and results to our headquarters for an annual contest. My accounting workshop won the international innovation award!

And it all started with a problem and what appeared to be a dumb idea to solve it.

Go figure.

Chapter 2

What Is "Hospitality Financial Leadership" Anyway?

A few years ago, finding the three words "hospitality financial leadership" together in one sentence wasn't possible. I know because I tried to Google them in 2014 and came up with a grab-bag of ideas on leadership, consulting, courses and more. Even the words "financial leadership" revealed surprisingly little—some tidbits about CEOs and their roles, but nothing any broader.

Yet in my opinion, financial leadership is the cornerstone of any manager, executive or leader's business acumen. It enables an individual to see the importance of being plugged into the strategy of the business, regardless of their given vocation or the industry they're in. They could be a human resources manager, a facilities manager, a chef or the head of an information technology division—but when they are financially tuned into the business at hand, they see the big picture. They know the role they play in delivering results and they can use their financial leadership skills to communicate with and lead their teams. They make the numbers in their world just as important as the other disciplines—like colleague engagement, service, and operations.

Financial leadership skills enable these managers to create a level of understanding and sophistication around business strategy. They can relate this understanding to the mission and vision of the team they're leading, all the way down to the contributions of individual team members. They see the numbers as a form of currency that provides fuel to ignite and mold the talent and collective efforts of their team.

The executive with financial leadership skills knows that the key ingredient each member of his or her squad needs to propel their individual careers is a sound grasp of the company and industry business strategy. Leaders enable financial leadership knowledge within their groups and, as a result, they produce other leaders who help propel the company's growth. Without these skills being brought out of the individuals by the functional leader, the contributions each person and the collective team can make are restricted.

In short, great leaders are developed, and they need exposure to the financials to grow. Hospitality Financial Leadership is the missing link for many hotel leaders and executives. It is hard to believe that some of our senior members are playing the game with a short hand. If you have been in hospitality for some time, you know exactly what I'm talking about. We promote people from Operations, Sales and other areas into the role of General Manager. It's been this way since the dawn of time. So, it's quite frightening to think that the hotel's most senior person, the one sitting in the pilot's seat, doesn't possess proper flying skills. In many cases they're just winging it. If the hotel owner knew just how green they were, he or she would slip a disk.

But you don't need to worry too much about the captain not knowing how to fly if they are open to learning financial leadership skills. This is where they can earn their wings.

Having the ability to manage people, the owner and the brand is key—but knowing how to make the numbers work is the nitro you *must* have if you're going to get off the ground and stay in the air.

What's the secret that will all but guarantee success?

Making the commitment to have the numbers be just another, equal part of what you do. This involves holding direct reports accountable for their departmental results on all levels. This means not giving anyone a pass when it comes to their budget just because they happen to also be valuable team members with amazing soft skills in their given area.

The committed leader doesn't blame the finance department when individual operating department numbers are upside down. Rather they are the quarterback who calls the plays. They make sure the forecasts and budgets come from the department managers—and not from the accounting department—because accurate, real-world numbers are needed for the smooth operation of a hotel. The finance/accounting department won't have those figures *unless individual departments turn them in.* But if they're not turned in, the finance department will need to make them up in order to create an operating budget. This is where a financial leader (a Controller or Director of Finance) is key. This man or woman of steel ensures each department head writes and owns their own monthly commentary. Our hero makes darn sure the daily communication around the numbers is consistent, positive, and clear. They make sure their team is provided with the resources and training they need to do this key job extremely well. And they take no prisoners. Blame and victims are not allowed on this ship.

That, my friends, is what Hospitality Financial Leadership is all about.

Watch this short video on "What is Financial Leadership?"

https://qrco.de/bd6YaG

Chapter 3

Engage Their Hearts and Minds First

You might think that getting your hotel leadership team excited about accounting is like convincing them it's fun to go to the dentist. Your average person wants nothing to do with it because they're predisposed to think it's potentially painful or boring. But once they begin to understand what the numbers mean and how to apply this understanding to general operations and the bottom line, they'll feel just the opposite.

Hotel leaders ALL want to have the financial wherewithal to dazzle their peers. They know it's the secret sauce to propel their careers and get them a seat at the captain's table. Participating in the inner financial circle is exciting and desirable.

Why, then, is there such a disconnect between a leader's desire to be financially astute and what often amounts to a complete lack of attention and discipline when it comes to the numbers? What is standing in the way of them embracing roles as financially savvy leaders?

There are several factors, all of which have everything to do with their approach to understanding the numbers.

1. **Level of understanding:** The numbers are confusing because the level of understanding is very low with most managers. It's not clear exactly how the individual numbers integrate with, apply to, and impact the hotel's performance.

2. **Someone else's job:** In most hotels, the numbers are viewed by the operational leaders as another person's responsibility. The typical departmental manager sees his or her role primarily in terms of serving hotel guests.

3. **No time:** Operational managers may feel they don't have the time to "look after" their numbers because they are already too busy with their guests and staff. The "administration stuff" is the last thing that gets their attention, with the result that the quality of the work and the level of their understanding of the numbers suffer.

4. **Not personally invested:** Leaders don't see a direct connection between their understanding of the numbers and their own personal prosperity.

What do we need to change to get the hotel management team to understand that the numbers are an important part of their responsibilities? How do we get them comfortable with and excited about building their financial acumen?

What you want to do is shift their perspective. You need to move away from the notion that the numbers are the hard part and embrace the idea that the numbers are awesome and represent the path to enhanced professionalism and personal success. Here are some ways to do this:

1. Educate: From day one, all leaders who have Profit and Loss responsibility should learn about the numbers. As early as the initial job interview, make sure any future employee in this field understands that respect for the numbers is a critical component of the hiring process—as much as their attention to service and engagement. And when someone new comes on board, make their ongoing education with the numbers as purposeful and routine as training in service and colleague engagement skills.

2. Make numbers a mainstay: Make the communication around numbers a daily and departmental mainstay. Every morning meeting and department briefing needs to include a review of how the current financial picture is shaping up. The communication needs to be fresh, informative and interesting. Simply regurgitating the latest occupancy and rate does nothing. We'll explore more about ways of communicating to your staff later in the book.

3. Attention: Ensure that your leaders all make and take the time to properly deal with their numbers. Focus your efforts on aligning a leader's responsibilities with the three equal pillars of service, engagement, and the numbers. When this balance is out of whack, corrections need to be made. We would not put up with a leader who is not pulling their weight with their service levels or colleague relations, and we should similarly address concerns about a lack of attention to the numbers.

4. Develop numbers acumen: Show your leaders that the numbers are not the hard part of hospitality. Let them see that having skills and developing acumen around the financial aspect of their career is powerful stuff. Show them that it's not difficult. Perhaps you are someone who remembers a time when you thought numbers were confusing and intimidating, but now you know better. Be the executive who leads their team in financial discipline. They will love you for making a difference in their world, and this is priceless experience for them—and for your own leadership.

5. Be realistic: Always remember that the numbers will never be perfect, and they will never go away. That sounds kind of scary and bleak—but that's the reality, and it's why appreciating the importance of the numbers is so key. We can take comfort in the fact that this imperfect yet relentless pursuit to be on top of things is in good company. People

would think you were crazy if you thought that service or staff engagement would be perfect in your hotel—but they would also think you were crazy if you didn't keep aiming high in these areas. With these two disciplines we accept the imperfection and come to work each day with a renewed determination to continually improve. The numbers should be treated in exactly the same way. They will never be perfect, and they will never go away. It's not like tenth-grade math— if I pass it, I will never have to deal with it again! The numbers are just how we keep score in the game of hotel management; they're simply another vital part of the business.

Once your managers see that the numbers are just as important as service and engagement, things will begin to shift. Even before they begin to improve their ability to communicate effectively around the financials, they'll start seeing the interplay of the numbers with other aspects of operations, and they'll likely find this very interesting. And as they settle into the process of taking the required time to manage their departmental finances, they will be proud of their accomplishment. Finally, once they realize that hotel financials are not so difficult, they will begin to teach others.

Your team of managers and leaders all want to have these skills and abilities—whether they know it or not!

What they're waiting for is you.

They need you to lead the way and "shift the perspective." Once you do, things will never be the same for you, your team, and your business.

Chapter 4

The Truth About Being a Financial Leader

The truth is that the team members and leaders in your hotel want to be financial leaders. They want to know, understand and speak properly about the numbers. They know it's the ticket to the big time, and that without financial skills and a solid understanding of the numbers they are not going to excel in their careers. It's that simple. They want to have the responsibility and the respect that comes with the financial badge.

Your job is to encourage this and make sure they get the right tools and messaging for the job. And this works for you too. Without broad participation, you're left with a team that has no financial helm. And don't think that that financial leadership will automatically come from the finance department—that notion is left for the amateurs. Getting people on board takes a leader with a vision that encompasses all the moving parts of your hotel's operations.

So where does your team go to get these skills? Sure, school is a great place to start, but we all know there's a big difference between what we learn in school and what we learn in the real world. The truth is that the best place to teach the operational financial piece is in the laboratory.

That laboratory is your hotel.

How do you train your leaders in the financials? Walk them through a variety of experiments. Explore the proper way to forecast staffing and expenses. Show them how they can wrap their arms around their piece. Slow things down and teach your leaders what they need to know about their numbers. It's not difficult to accomplish. It just takes a little time, preparation, and dedication.

The same holds true if you're a leader who wants to learn the financials yourself. Work with your hotel. Share that you recognize the importance of learning to work with the numbers for yourself and for the hotel. Most likely you will be rewarded with increased opportunities. And if you're told to "mind your own business"—well, that just might give you a clue about the potential for upward mobility at your hotel.

Like learning anything else in our world, the process of coming to grips with the financial piece will take a little time and effort, but it's a growth process that will benefit anyone who engages with it. We tend to think the subject of numbers is somehow different because money has power—power that is often used to intimidate and scare. Instead, show your leaders that money is just another piece of the puzzle that we can figure out and manage.

When we treat the financials as just another part of our business that we can tame and master, our team sees this and they get on board. But if we treat the financial piece like it's oxygen and in scarce supply, we give it a bad reputation. Who would want to get into that business if they believed that sooner or later it would blow up in their faces? That's the kind of financial leadership scare tactic we want to avoid.

We all know we will drop the ball at some point in our hotels with service and employee engagement—and more often than we might care to admit. That's a given, and we accept the fact that we're not machines, and we're not perfect. The hotel business is not a science. It's an art. And when we drop the ball, we just need to pick it up again. We learn what didn't work, fix it, and move on. This attitude is vital—whether you're teaching or learning.

There are always challenges to work on. The money needs the

same loving care and understanding as everything else does. When we use the power of money to scare, threaten and intimidate, we're just shooting ourselves in the foot. If you're in a leadership position, you need to let the people you're instructing know that you'll be there when they screw up, and you will help them get it right. Just like you do with their guests and colleagues. We're all works-in-progress.

When we give the money piece the same attention and understanding that we give to other areas, people give it the focused workout it needs to get in shape. When the whole team exercises their financial pieces together, the hotel "body" gets really fit. And like rowers in a crew race, the efficiency and speed your team can generate together is much more powerful than a single oarsman. The financial leader you want to be is the one who has a plan to include all the members of your leadership team who have profit and loss responsibilities. That's a big group, including all your department managers and assistants. So your plan should include training and development that gives the money the same level of focus as guest service and colleague engagement.

Chapter 5

Shift Your Thinking

We all have predisposed ways that we look at our world and the things, people, and circumstances inside of it. It's what makes us human and we either have an open mind or one that's closed. Another way to express this is that we either have a fixed mindset or a growth mindset.

In her wonderful book *Mindset*, Carol Dweck dives deep into this distinction and relates it to our lives. I highly recommend reading her book—it's nothing short of amazing. In this chapter I am going to apply this distinction to you and your hotel career. Specifically, around the notion that someone is either a numbers person or not.

When I start a financial leadership workshop, I invite the participant to shift their thinking—to shift from the idea they had before they got there. They had probably been thinking something like, "Ugh. We're going to have to sit through a boring session on accounting and numbers." I invite them to shift their thinking to curiosity, to learning, to developing a new understanding and skillset that will help grow their career and abilities. As a result, they will likely have greater career success.

I typically get a few smiles, but for the most part I see puzzled expressions. Perplexed looks, because most people don't buy into or believe that something they hold onto so tightly could be just the opposite. That's because they have a fixed mindset.

With a fixed/closed mindset, people are trapped with their ego or self-belief. The ironclad idea that what they have right now, in this very moment, is all they need. Even more, and, most importantly, it's not worth it to look for another opinion or way of looking at something. To them it literally means that another way would mean their way was tantamount to failure, that they are ill-equipped—and that feeling must be avoided at all costs. They protect their fragile view of themselves and the world they inhabit at all costs because it's safe to do so. I guess you could say that this type of person might be the one who already knows it all. Do you know what I mean?

With an open/growth mindset, people see their current position or idea as simply a starting point. One that can and should be altered with new information, ideas, ways of doing and ways of being. They see opportunities and they're willing to admit that they need to work on themselves and their abilities to advance. They are not afraid of looking like they are not 100% ready or already fully equipped. They are open to the learning and growth opportunities in front of them because they see the upside of doing this. They approach new ideas and different information with a sense of excitement and adventure. You might say this type of person is a keener or fast learner when in fact they're just trying to improve their lives. They will readily admit they don't know everything about anything.

Let's get back to the notion that you are a hotel numbers person or not. With a closed mindset you see the numbers as someone else's deal. "That's an accounting responsibility, and not mine." Closed mindset people don't see the opportunity in learning more about how the numbers relate to them because it would mean that they need help. They certainly won't step up and dig in because that would ultimately mean they possess some deficiency.

With a growth, open or learning mindset, people see the circumstances before them as an invitation to get involved and even mess things up a bit. They see the opportunity in the chaos. What they get back by getting involved is the reward of being the one who figured it out, turned it around, and finally drained the swamp. It's just another part of what they do. They see the career advancement potential and they go for it. All in.

The person with an open mind is not better than the person with a closed mind. They're just more fun to be around sometimes. A person who is predisposed to NOT trying new, previously uncharted things runs the risk of being a little boring.

Having a closed mindset does not mean you can't change it; it just means you are going to need to be okay with failure. In the failure you will learn and grow. In the failure you will succeed.

Trying and not knowing how it will turn out is the difference maker. Trying and failing means you will try again and succeed. Remember how you learned to ride a bike?

Mastering your numbers requires failure. The hotel business can feel like it's just one failure after another—until it isn't anymore.

Watch a short video on "Shift Your Thinking"

https://qrco.de/bd6YEc

Chapter 6

Why Financial Acumen (aka Leadership) Is so Important to Your Hospitality Career

It is common sense: With more knowledge and skills, your career prospects and advancement possibilities are enhanced. In hospitality, as it's related to the financials, this commonsense idea is not quite as well understood.

There exists a counterculture to growing up in our business, to raising oneself out of the guest and colleague-only world into the financial arena. I know and have met many people who camp out in hospitality to avoid the numbers; this may be one of the reasons why they got into the industry in the first place—they didn't want to deal with the "hard facts" of business. But to advance in hospitality you need to know your numbers.

The hotel world has changed tremendously in the past twenty to forty years. I have been at it for forty-plus years, and the most profound change I see is a movement away from the brands, aka the owner/operator model, to one where most hotel companies became management companies, or franchises. In simple terms, this means the name on the door forty years ago was the owner of the bricks and mortar. Today the name on the door, nineteen times out of twenty, simply means the brand has a management or franchise agreement with the hotel owner or owners. What this translates to—as far as how the hotel is run— is where we have all seen and felt the changes.

The old model had a much kinder and gentler approach to fostering a culture of inclusion, family, longevity, and a strong service culture. I distinctly remember my first stint in a "managed hotel" inside my company. People had warned me that it was different, and they were right. The owned hotels had a clear sense of togetherness, and you knew what was important. I grew up with this slogan in my DNA, "Look after the guests and the money looks after itself." When I left the safety of the owned nest, I learned a few new things.

The owner in my new, managed hotel needed a certain return each quarter to meet his debt and investor obligations. Back home in the owner/operator model this was never a topic of discussion. It seemed head office was always grumpy about the results but never spoke of external obligations. These new owner obligations had a profound effect on how we operated, especially the first year I was at the managed hotel.

Things started out bad and were not going well at my first managed hotel.

We missed the first two quarters and immediate action ensued. Staffing and expense reviews had a level of focus I had never seen before on department managers being accountable for their monthly forecasts and the results. We scheduled F&B outlet days and hours using occupancy by transient and groups to determine demand. We designed and implemented a staffing guide of all scheduled positions. Each manager was accountable for their schedule based on an approved formula. No more looking after our colleagues in the low occupancy periods. This was a luxury we could not afford. We tore apart the food cost and especially the buffet offerings, and designed menus that reflected business levels. Back at the ranch, there was never a focus like this.

In all, my experience with my first managed hotel was very positive. As luck would have it, business really picked up after my second quarter there, and for the next two years our team enjoyed great results. Our owner's rep (today's version of an asset manager) was happy and more than willing to invest. This was another point of sharp contrast to the old homestead reality. At the owned hotels, money came for capital on a regular train, regardless of the results. In the new world, we saw the intent and the desire for investment as a clear link to our ability to generate a return.

So how does this relate to you and your financial acumen? Simple: you are in a business that now needs you to operate as a businessperson. Just like my story of going from the safety of the owned into the new world of the managed hotel, your career will be greatly enhanced by getting your financial leadership game on. Perhaps you just made a move to a new position or hotel and the demands and expectations are a little different.

Don't turn from that light—do the opposite:

Run straight at it!

Maybe your new role is a little scary and has a sharper focus on profit performance. Do not worry—that is par for the course today. Owners need to make their numbers. Your job now is to deliver. Your tools are the same as mine were. Get to know your costs and how to flex them.

Once these tools are in place, your job is to make sure the other managers and leaders in your business all buy in and use them.

Watch a short video on "The Best Hotel Career Advice"

https://qrco.de/bd6fzJ

Chapter 7

She Said She Was Born Without the Financial Gene

The following is a recap of a single coaching session which turned into a coaching relationship with a client.

I am going to call my client Jennifer.

I was speaking at a local hotel association event and as usual a few people came to see me at the end to share their thoughts. Jennifer was the very last person to speak with me. She waited until the room was almost empty. She was shy and nervous.

"I just want to thank you," she said.

"Thank me for what?" I replied.

"Thank you for giving me some hope."

I smiled, as I knew exactly what she meant, but I still said, "Hope for what?"

She explained how terrified she was about the financials in her hotel and how the director of finance made everything so complicated. She continued with how the weekly department head meetings were awful, because during them there was a chance she would get asked about her department's results. She was completely embarrassed when having to speak about the numbers. She then explained how she was somehow born without the financial gene, but now she was responsible for her department's numbers, and she was sure that her career was doomed.

I smiled, because I have heard this story a thousand times. Always a little different, but it contains the same elements. "Me and numbers just don't work. Somehow, I was shortchanged at birth and I'm not a numbers person. I love my job, but the numbers are the tough part."

I listened openly, and then I asked her *the* question. I love asking this question.

I asked her, "Why do you think the numbers are so difficult for you?"

To which she replied, "I don't know; they're just so complicated and intimidating."

I replied, "I don't believe you. All you're missing is a little practice."

She laughed and said, "No, you don't understand: me and numbers just don't work."

We talked a bit more and I offered her a telephone call the following week to discuss her challenges with numbers. She said she would like that. I asked her to send me the latest financial statement (P&L) for her department.

To which she replied, "I'm not sure I'm allowed to send it to you."

"Not to worry," I replied. "Talk to your boss." A few days later, after she got permission to send me the material, I received the financial statement, and then we had our call.

When we started, I asked Jennifer to tell me about her career path. She explained that she went to college and studied art history and found a summer job as a guest services agent to help with the school bills. One thing led to another, and she was promoted to a Reception Manager position, and most recently to the position of Front Office Manager. She explained to me that she loved her job, the customers and the staff—but hated the numbers.

"Okay," I said. "I get it that the numbers are the hard part for you. But what if they were not the hard part? What if they were just another part of your job? How would things be different for you if that was the case?"

She laughed and said, "If the numbers were just another part of my job I would be in heaven."

"Alright then let's have a look at things," I said. "Let's start with the top-level statement." This was the September financial statement. "Okay: first lesson. The hotel financial statement is organized just like the hotel. It starts with a summary statement and then: Rooms, Food and Beverages (F&B), Minor Operating Departments, Non-Operating Departments, all leading up to the Gross Operating Profit. Each part of the big statement ties back to the corresponding lines on the summary statement. There is the current month on the left and the year-to-date (YTD) on the right. The year-to-date includes all the activity accumulated for the year, including September.

"Let's look at the sales department as an example. Find the sales statement," I said.

We both went to page thirty.

"Find the total payroll," I asked her.

She said, "$12,542, and YTD $118,988."

"OK," I said. "Go back to the summary and find the sales department and the payroll line. See, it's the same number in both the month and YTD columns."

We repeated this exercise for each line of the summary statement. This took about twenty minutes. When we were done with this, I asked her if this exercise was helpful.

"Yes!" She said enthusiastically. "I never knew how the whole statement tied together."

With this exercise now complete I asked her if she understood the purpose of the profit and loss statement (P&L). When she said, "Yes," I asked her to describe that purpose. She replied quite clearly that the purpose of the P&L was to highlight the revenues, expenses, and profits. She went on to explain that the statement was used to keep track of the financial results, the good and the bad.

"Exactly," I said.

I mentioned that the statement we were looking at was the September P&L. I then asked her what the statement told us about

October?

She was quiet for just a second and then said, again very clearly, "Nothing. We have a different report that comes out each month called the forecast. It would show us the same information not for September but for the next 3 months."

"Well then," I said, "You just explained the difference between the actual and forecast reports."

She laughed and said, "I guess I understand a little more than I thought."

We both laughed, and I said, "You sound like you're ready to learn about the balance sheet and how the P&L and balance sheet work together."

"Balance sheet," she moaned, "I have looked at that before and it's so confusing."

I replied, "It's actually so simple to understand. I bet you I can teach it to you in the next fifteen minutes."

Attached at the end of the September P&L was the balance sheet summary report for September. I asked her to get a piece of paper and a pen.

"Write the following," I said. "Let's pretend you own a home and it's worth $500,000, and you have a mortgage on that house for $400,000. Write down those two items and tell me the difference between the two."

She said, "$100,000."

"Exactly," I said. "Your house is the asset, the mortgage is your liability and the difference, the $100,000, is your equity."

That three-part formula is the way the balance sheet works. It's the same in every business regardless of its size, industry, or complexity. It's the universal formula for accounting and it's called the fundamental accounting equation. I told her to write down the formula. Assets equals liabilities plus equity ($A = L + E$).

One other thing about the formula you need to understand is that the equity can be negative as well.

"Imagine," I said, "If you owned that house in 2008 and its value had dropped to $350,000 and you still had a $400,000 mortgage, how much would your equity be?"

She paused for just a second and said, "$50,000."

And I said, "It would be -$50,000."

"OK, I get it," she said. "But how does this relate to the balance sheet?"

I explained that the balance sheet has the same three parts.

First the assets. I asked her to review the list on the summary statement we both had.

"What's the first asset listed?" I said.

"Cash," was her reply.

"What's next?" I asked.

"Guest ledger," she replied. "I have seen that before and I wanted to ask what it was, but I was too embarrassed."

I replied, "Imagine all the guests in your hotel gathering at the same time in the lobby, each holding a sign with a number on it. That number is the amount they owe the hotel; add them all up, and that's the guest ledger."

We quickly reviewed the rest of the assets, and we noted the total assets: $9,235,526.

"Write that number down," I said.

Second, it's the liabilities. We reviewed the liabilities. I asked her what liabilities she had.

She laughed and then said, "You mean what bills do I need to pay?"

"Yes," I said. "What obligations do you have that you must pay?"

She replied that she had a car loan, a utility bill, and a student loan. Those are obligations you have that you cannot skip out on. The liabilities that the hotel has are the same idea. We then reviewed the list and, like with the assets, we noted the total liabilities, and I asked her to write that number down: $8,300,291

"What's the difference between the two numbers?" I asked.

A few seconds later she said, "$935,235."

I asked her to tell me the "equity" to which she replied, "It's the same number: $935,235."

Assets 9,235,526 = Liabilities 8,300,291 + Equity 935,235 (A = L + E)

"One last thing before we wrap up this lesson," I said. "Go back to the summary P&L and find the line that says net income."

I waited for probably thirty seconds and then she gave me the number.

"OK, so next I want you to look at the equity section on the balance sheet again, and I want you to find that same number."

Five seconds later she said, "Current period retained earnings—it's the same number!"

That is how the P&L and the balance sheet are tied together; the total of all the revenues less all the expenses is net income on the P&L, and current period retained earnings on the balance sheet.

To wrap up the lesson I asked her to explain the relationship between the P&L and the balance sheet in her own words.

She said, after a brief pause, "The P&L is like my wages, less all the deductions and my living expenses, and the balance sheet is like my bank account and savings. If there is money left over from my pay after all that's taken into account, that's my equity."

"That's a pretty good analogy," I said.

At that moment we both knew that the tough part was not so tough. Like anything in life, she just needed a little practice, and having a coach to help her just made the task a lot easier and much faster.

Chapter 8

Nobody Gets to Be Wrong

"Nobody gets to be wrong; everybody is wrong. Nobody gets to be right; everybody is right."

I use this quote to start many of my workshops. To me, it's the way I want the participants to stand in their individual power during our time together. It's also how I see our industry. In the hotel business, we all need to have an opinion, and even more importantly we need to be able to share it. This is because we all have something important to bring to the table.

To illustrate this, I often ask the following question:

"What would you rather have to increase your Gross Operating Profit (GOP) in your 300-room hotel, which is currently operating at 75% occupancy with a $150 average rate:

1) a $4 room rate increase?

or

2) two more points of occupancy?"

I get a lot of responses right off the bat. People are quick to jump on both options. But which one is right? The simple answer is that they're both right—and at the same time they're both wrong.

That's the way I see it, anyway. Our business is not a science where there is a definitive answer. I have always said, "Put ten hotel people in a room, ask one question, and you will get at least twelve answers."

Hotel people love to pontificate about the answer to just about any question involving operations or the finances of hotels. You're never really short of opinions on what you should do, or what it means. That's the way it is with most hotel leaders. What I want is the same level of bravado in *all* the participants in my workshop session. So, to stir things up a bit with the audience, this is what I like to do.

Typically all the participants will have an opinion, but they are often hesitant to share it right away. Many of the workshop attendees are not used to being in the spotlight or on a stage. Just like the audience at a talk show, they need to be properly warmed up before we can get the most from them.

So I say something like this:

Depending upon where you work in your hotel, you will probably have a different opinion about what you would like better—an increase in the rate or the occupancy. Let's play this out a bit longer and do some math on each option to see if one selection is better than the other when it comes to GOP.

- A $4 increase in rate seems like a no brainer. We all like rate because it's almost all pure profit.
  - A 300-room hotel * 365 days = 109,500 rooms available over the course of a year
  - Currently operating at 75% = (109,500 * .75 = 82,125 rooms sold)
  - Add $4.00 for each of those 82,125 rooms over the course of a year and you get a significant amount of new room revenue ($4.00 * 82,125 = $328,500). Less some additional online travel agent commissions, corporate fees, credit card commissions and we're left with, say, 90% of that (328,500 *.90) = **$295,650 in additional GOP**
- 2 points of occupancy can also sound attractive.
  - 109,500 rooms available over the course of a year. 109,500 * .02 = 2,190 additional rooms. (2,190 * $150 average room rate = $328,500) in new room

revenue. Less the additional costs for commissions, cleaning and amenities for the occupied rooms and the additional fees and credit card commissions at 30% = ($328,500 *.70) = **$229,950 in additional GOP**

At this point, I say something like, "So I guess the room rate scenario wins; is there anything else we need to consider?" It usually takes about two seconds before the questioning starts.

- "What if the new rooms are group rooms?"
- "What if the additional rate comes from the OTAs?" (Online travel agencies that can take additional fees)
- "What if the new occupancy is on Sundays?"
- "What if the additional rate comes from existing corporate clients?"
- "What if the additional occupancy comes from transient family clients?"
- "What about the additional wear and tear on our rooms with that extra occupancy?"
- "What if we had some of both occupancy and rate? What would that look like?"

By this time, we have a full-on debate raging and everyone seems to have opinions—some of which are held very strongly. The foodies have one slant, and the salespeople have another. Rooms people are all about having the "right" customers staying in our rooms. The administration folks can make the argument either way. The GM says she would take either scenario with a smile. Eventually I chime in and make my point: in our business, we can all see things our own way. We can justify almost anything as it relates to what's good or not so good for our business.

Knowing this about the people in the workshop is a good place to start. Showing them that their opinion counts and that it's just as valid as another person's is a powerful exercise. I want people to see that they make a difference no matter where in the hotel they earn their paycheck. We're all in this together, and whether the subject is more business, right-sizing the employee headcount or what's for lunch in the cafeteria, everyone is entitled to their own thoughts.

Nobody gets to be wrong; everybody is wrong. Nobody gets to be right; everybody is right.

If we can truly model this philosophy, then we can get the entire team to lean into the challenge of figuring out this thing we call hotel management. What is the best way to move forward? There are so many aspects of the business we need to attend to. What can we do to truly engage the hearts and minds of the entire team?

That's what it's all about: getting everyone to play. If we sit on the sidelines waiting for the GM and corporate to fill our heads with what to do and how to think, we've just ordered the worst dish on the menu. Be a hotel full of the mindset that it's all about having everyone step up and truly contribute.

Chapter 9

Welcoming Imperfection

If you're a leader in hospitality and you want to wrap your arms around the numbers, I have some advice.

To maximize effective leadership around money, accept the fact that working with the numbers is an endless exercise. The idea of "mastering" the numbers is something of a fantasy. The figures are always changing—that's the nature of the game. It's a little like trying to mark your place on the surface of running water.

It's critical to remember that when we do a budget or forecast for our hotel, or for a specific department in it, the only thing we know for certain is that it's *wrong*.

Yes, wrong. It will never be absolutely right.

Why do we go through such an exercise if we know it's wrong? Simply because we want a system that produces information about where our business is going so we can manage it accordingly. We get a snapshot of a moving picture—the flow of numbers. It's never quite complete, and the reality is always changing. But it can still inform our next steps. Understanding this means we don't have to seek the "holy grail" of our numbers being perfect.

Oddly enough, this idea of inevitable imprecision is in great company in the hotel world. Meet money's two sisters: guest services and colleague engagement.

Together, these three pillars of hotel operations function in the same fashion.

Guest service is a constant, never-ending battle in our hotels. We accept the fact that it will never be mastered. There will always be challenges:

- Training
- Maintaining standards
- New colleagues
- Technology glitches
- Communication issues
- Guest expectations
- Business volumes
- Staffing challenges
- Value for money

. . . and so on. Knowing the job will never be mastered keeps us on our game. Hospitality and service are not absolutes, and running a hotel is not a science. There is an endless list of ingredients and conditions that produce a different result every single time. That's our business. What we need to do is accept the challenge—meet it head-on and perform.

Similarly, colleague engagement is the never-ending practice of building a team to take on the challenges of our business. Creating and maintaining an engaged team in your hotel facilitates the delivery of quality service. This is another process that will never be complete. There will always be:

- Turnover
- Lack of turnover
- Staffing level challenges
- Business volumes
- Staffing shortages
- Resource issues
- Communication issues

- Last-minute changes

Once again, I could fill this page and so could you with all the colleague engagement challenges we have. And again, what's most important is that we accept the fact that the colleague engagement job is never done. We don't give up and we fight every day to improve the landscape and win.

The *real* task at hand is to create a business plan through which we achieve a superior financial result. Having and executing such a plan helps us direct resources to execute our mission. With the plan in hand, every department can take its best shot. That's exactly what we want them to do. Know the target, take the shot. Hit or miss, just take the shot.

Knowing there will be new challenges tomorrow keeps us excited to see what shows up. It's comparable to playing a team sport where we get a chance to win every day. And even if we win, our performance is full of areas we could have executed better. Then we come back the next day and play again. This is the essence of our business.

The reward comes from moving the needle in the right direction, providing the best services, building the best team and, ultimately, creating a successful business.

Watch a short video about "Welcoming Imperfection"

https://qrco.de/bd6Z1C

Chapter 10

Flying By the Seat of Your Pants

In most hotels, the system for forward-looking financial management is nonexistent. We rely on the top line coming in, and if it does, we expect a certain profit picture to emerge. When revenues are good this works—sometimes. When revenues do not materialize because of an event or something that produces headwinds in our business, we almost always fall flat on our face as regards desired profitability.

This is flying by the seat of your pants. We think we have no way of knowing what is really going to happen financially in our business. We roll the dice every month. When we are in a fly-by-the-seat-of-our-pants hotel and we have a good month, things are great, but we really do not know why. For example, why were expenses so low this month? Or perhaps payroll seems too good to be true. When we have a bad month, the sins are obvious: missed invoices from prior periods, over-forecast in payroll, and revenues below forecast. Didn't anyone see this coming? Well, actually, no. No one saw this coming because we do not have a financial communication process to ensure we are on top of the business.

When we are in a fly-by-the-seat-of-our-pants hotel and we have a bad result the GM points fingers at the controller. The controller blames the department heads who didn't submit their forecast on time. The department heads blame the controller because he/she created the forecast anyway! You see, it just goes around and around. No accountability, no ownership, lousy results, and no financial leadership!

This is a dangerous and irresponsible practice that almost always leads to financial failure. It is a common practice in our industry, and one that has led to many financial meltdowns. For some, the argument would be that the finance department is responsible for managing the numbers. That might sound like the right idea to the layman, but in practice it is short-sighted. It rarely works, because the finance department has no real way of knowing what is going on in the various departments within the hotel.

The fact is, the accounting department's job is to record what happened, capture the data in the month *for* the month, report the results, and ensure the assets and liabilities are properly recorded and safeguarded. It's *not* its job to know what each area in the hotel will do next month, next quarter, next year. If we want that kind of forward-looking intelligence in our hotel, we need to create a system to generate it. What can we do to create this system? Keep reading because it's coming to you!

If we want to have a system in our hotel that allows us to manage the financial picture properly, we need to give our managers and leaders the responsibility for their results—which means they need to create their own budgets and forecasts. They need to know what is in the middle of their statements.

Stop flying by the seat of your pants and get your financial leadership on!

Watch a short video on "Flying by the Seat of Your Pants"

https://qrco.de/bd6gQ6

Chapter 11

The Three Pillars of Hospitality

As I mentioned earlier, in the hotel business, there are three pillars: the guests, the colleagues and the money. They are not equal. Period, full stop!

They are not equal because we ignore the third—financial—pillar, and we do so at our own peril. This chapter will show you what is possible when we step up, and it points you to a fantastic model that can have your owner happily paying for the whole deal. (The scenario I'm laying out here applies to a branded, managed property—not a franchised or owner-operated hotel.)

Pillar 1 – Guest Service

We manage guest interaction with an understanding and belief that we are all invested in good guest service. Even the departments that do not have direct guest contact help support the colleagues and departments that do. We are all responsible. Good guest service is a no-brainer for anyone in the hotel business. It is the very moral foundation that our business is built upon.

Finding ways to increase guest service is just good business. We invest in guest service at all levels in our hotels and we take the function of providing great service very seriously. In branded managed hotels, the management company typically has guest service programs they have either created or they provide.

In addition, we spend serious dollars asking our guests how we are doing. Guest service scores are critical to the operations of the hotel. In every instance the brand mandates the guest service programs inside their hotels and the owners pay 100% of the tab for everything related to creating and maintaining guest service. Many owners question the management company's programs, which can be very expensive and have results that are hard to nail down.

Annually, the brand will send their hotels the yearly programs via budget documents that outline all the programs the hotel needs to add to their upcoming year. Even if the hotel adds labor for training, the owner, in the end, pays 100%. When you think about a brand and its service reputation, it is interesting to see through this mirage—to look and see that ultimately the owners of the hotels are paying to create the brand's service promise.

This is largely a secret to most people. Understanding the relationship between the brand, the owner and what is created via this dance can be very illuminating. In most branded managed hotels, the annual guest service score forms part of the executive team's bonus criteria and achieving the targeted number or better is a direct link to their pocketbooks.

Pillar 2 – Colleague Engagement

With colleague engagement, it is the same: We are all involved and implicated in managing departments and creating hotel teams that have high colleague engagement. No leader or department manager is excused from the mission of colleague engagement.

We have a myriad of tools to engage the staff, from employee newsletters, town halls, monthly colleague meetings, seasonal parties, special celebrations, sports teams, long service awards, employee of the year, employee opinion surveys, whistle-blower lines, employee assistance programs, employee benefits, employee meals, etc. I could go on and on—this list is very long. The irony in all of this is that the owner pays 100% of the cost of any and every program or event. Once again, this dynamic between the brand and the owner is an interesting dance to watch. Owners question many expenses related to "creating" colleague engagement, but in the end, they pay.

So, what is the benefit of good employee engagement? It is obvious: good engagement coupled with great service equals a fantastic opportunity for our guests to have a wonderful experience.

It used to be the case that human resources were "responsible" for creating colleague engagement, but not any longer. Each department has its own employee opinion survey score and a bad apple in the bag will not last long. No leader is excused from the necessity of great colleague engagement.

Pillar 3 – The Money

The money, the P&L, the owner—it all boils down to the same thing: providing a superior return for the shareholder. How is this pillar different? Well, really it is *not* different. We just treat it differently.

When we talk about the money and ask ourselves what we do to create financial leadership inside of our hotels, the answer nineteen times out of twenty is NOTHING. We do nothing to lead and educate our management teams on the matter of financial skills.

I am not talking about the accounting department and the financial function. I am talking about the education and the skills of the non-financial leaders in our hotels. What do we do inside our hotels to create management teams that have a solid financial foundation? **The answer: NOTHING.** (Though I hope this book changes your approach!)

Why might you be asking is this the case? There are three reasons that I will point out:

1. We still live in an owner/operator mindset that echoes the idea, "Look after the guests and the money will look after itself." But the reality today is that we manage hotels, and as a management company we sell expertise to owners. Brands need to slow down long enough to realize they need to evolve beyond creating additional brand options and invest and develop their leadership ranks.

2. The finances and talking about the money for many people is still taboo. The idea that we share the P&L and the managers get to see the financial results is upsetting a sacred cow for many people. To this notion I can only say, "Get over it." If we want to have mature, responsible leaders, we need to trust them and share the financial information.

3. We seemingly do not know how to lead and educate our managers financially. We hide behind the numbers and push them off as the responsibility of the finance department. This is really the opportunity in all of this. We have the ability to train

and lead our managers financially, and this is not difficult to accomplish. **In fact, the owner will pay 100% of the cost to create the financial leadership in your hotel.** Just as we discussed in the other two pillars, the brand can mandate the training program and the owner will pay 100% of the cost.

Leaders want to be educated financially and they want to have financial responsibility. The idea that leaders do not want to do this work is nonsense. Today's leaders are dying to get financial leadership skills. They know without these abilities their careers are limited.

There are some conditions to this.

Leaders (of departments and so on) need to know you are there to support them, to provide the education and the training to facilitate the creation of financial leadership as part of your culture. Giving your leadership the responsibility for the numbers is not enough—you need to give them a system and be there when it counts. Be there when it is a mess and support their efforts. Be there when it is a win and celebrate their success. The brand and the general manager need to get behind this initiative. It is not a finance and accounting function, it is one of the three pillars, and it is a front-line management function for every single leader. It is not someone else's responsibility.

Hiding out behind the numbers is not a viable strategy. Leaders need to know you have a system for them to follow, a predictable process with defined timelines and accountability for all. Leaders want to produce their own budgets and forecasts, not be given numbers that someone else has cooked up and told, "Good luck—here are your numbers."

Leaders need to see that you are investing in them, in their career and in their success. Once they see you are committed to their success, it is a game changer. If they sense that you're offering anything less, you will not succeed.

The Benefits of Financial Leadership Are Everywhere

Leaders who know what is happening financially in their departments can plan and execute better.

Imagine a leader who knows their expenses and payroll, and he or she tracks the sales and volumes in the month and adjusts spending and schedules accordingly.

The brand also benefits from financial leadership training, building bench strength as leaders move throughout the organization. A brand with this kind of talent will quickly make a name for itself.

The owner benefits big time. Having a financially engaged leadership team means the team is all in when it comes to maximizing resource and profits.

We all know that in our industry we have a million ways to waste money. On the flip side, with a financially engaged team we have a million ways to *save* money.

It is all about the culture you create, and it can be fun!

Like building a great service culture or a colleague engagement machine, financially engaged leadership teams are every bit as possible.

How do you grow a garden? You plant seeds and you nurture and care for them.

The financial leadership piece in your hotel is exactly the same.

Chapter 12

The How-to versus the Want-to

The business of managing hotel finances is not terribly technical or complicated. What makes it challenging is that it's usually a very *large* job involving many people. In a 500-room hotel, you can easily have 20+ forecast contributors. The communication system in the hotel is the key to both smooth management and predictive financial results. This is the "how-to."

If hotel finances are not a complicated matter, then why is it such a challenge in so many hotels? The answer lies in finding the "want-to."

Most leaders in the hotel don't naturally want to be managing numbers. They typically didn't get into the hotel business with the idea that they would be businesspeople with forecasts and budgets to run. They're "people people"—artists and creators. We all know the stories of how so many of us found our way into hospitality and fell in love. Most of your non-financial leaders landed in hospitality for a short stay and decided to move in. Now, a few years later, they find themselves in roles with responsibilities to get the numbers done, and they don't like it.

They don't like it for a few reasons:

1. They are often responsible for numbers that are created by someone else, someone who expects that leader to own the numbers. This rarely happens. If you're cooking up the numbers in your hotel and giving them to your department

managers, then stop! This is a complete waste of time as they will not take any ownership with these targets—they're yours, not theirs. Know that the other leaders are quietly thumbing their nose at you when you do this. You're placing a huge expectation on them and they don't like it one little bit.

2. They don't have a good financial communication system to use when dealing with the numbers. Non-financial leaders need a strong schedule and constant communication around the numbers. It's not enough to publish daily reports and expect that the managers will read and use them. You need to have the numbers be an integral part of the daily communication system in the hotel. Not just arrivals and departures, VIP's, outlet hours and groups in-house at your daily meetings. You need to shine a light on yesterday's revenues, month-to-date revenues and the variance to forecast. Every day your leaders should know if we're on track to make our top line and divisional revenues. If not, then how will they be able to react and adjust labor and spending to compensate and affect the flow?

3. They don't take the time necessary to properly manage the numbers. Your leaders will always treat the numbers as second unless you show them that the numbers are just as important as the guests and their colleagues. How do you do that? Simple: make the numbers real and treat the leaders as adults who have financial power. Invite them into the captain's lounge and show them the respect you have for their role. Be there and be supportive and helpful when things are not going well, and be there to celebrate and encourage when times are good. We all know our business has ups and downs and that it's cyclical in nature, so be the kind of leader who walks the talk and knows it's not always easy for your leaders. Have respect for their challenges.

How Can We Create the Want-to?

The want-to do this in all of these areas is naturally low. Let's be realistic for a moment and ask ourselves: "If they really wanted to manage their expenses and know how much they spent, they could figure it out; so how do we increase the want-to?" We do this by showing our leaders what is possible with good financial communication by investing in financial leadership in our hotel. Leaders realize very quickly that it's not so complicated, and mastering the numbers is 100% possible.

Your leaders really want to be responsible for their numbers. I am going to tell you why this is the case, but first, a little story to reinforce the how-to versus want-to distinction.

A few years ago, our daughter moved in with Johanne and I while we were living in San Francisco. She had finished university and had come home to start her career and was staying with us until she got on her feet. One thing developed that we were not anticipating. She was a messy housekeeper and her room was a disaster. I asked her several times to clean it up and somehow this just wasn't working.

Now, in this situation, it would never dawn on me to send her on a course to learn how to clean her room. She knows how to clean her room! So, what's missing? Answer: she doesn't *want to* clean her room. Period full stop. Doesn't want to. If I am going to have any impact on this situation, I need to operate in the realm of increasing the want-to. As author and coach Steve Chandler has pointed out, once someone, anyone, has an increase of "the want-to, the how-to is everywhere." (In the case of my daughter, our conversations led to a small improvement in housekeeping, but it wasn't until she got her own place that things really changed.)

Increasing the want-to is always the answer we seek. What's in it for them? What will be better in their lives that will make them motivated to do the task at hand? With financial leadership in your hotel, there are lots of areas in which you can cultivate the want-to.

Financial leadership skills are extremely valuable tools for your non-financial leaders to have. In today's competitive world it's not enough just to be great with the guests and colleagues. Leaders need these financial skills to advance. All your leaders want to move ahead. They all want to be executives and lead. When you present these as opportunities, your leaders will happily step up. We also must remember that the only place your leaders can get these skills from is you. They need you to create the environment that nurtures these skills. Your leaders see more dollars in their pockets, and rightly so: with these skills they are much more valuable.

Your leaders all want to have more impact. Once you show your team what happens with their numbers and how they directly affect the business, and that all stakeholders are directly impacted by their efforts, they are going to naturally want to get on board. Maslow's hierarchy of needs shines a light on people wanting respect for their work and to have a meaningful role to play. When framed properly this is incredibly powerful. Self-esteem and self-actualization are direct by-products of having financial leadership skills and responsibilities.

This comes with a warning label. Make the responsibilities a positive attribute and not one that is negative. Management by embarrassment will backfire big time, every time. The financial leadership in your hotel needs to always be packaged with love, and never fear. If we put fear and money in the same boat, we are sunk.

When you train and invest in financial leadership you slow things down with the financial piece, and the byproduct of this is that your managers will see it's not complicated. Getting your leaders in the same room to study the P&L and how things come together financially in all the different departments is magic. The curtain falls and your team will stop believing it's a difficult subject because they all see this together. When a chef explains his labor expenditures and sales managers talk about their expenses, the whole room now has a new window into the story, and the mystery evaporates before their eyes. By teaching our leaders we show them the real story around the numbers, and this cannot be accomplished without slowing down and taking the time to learn. Just like service training or engagement. We need to invest in what we want to grow. Regular, ongoing creative training around the finances drives the want-to.

The last part of the want-to is my favorite. Why would I want to have a financially engaged team in my hotel? Don't forget to check in on your own want-to as well as that of your leaders. I want to have a financially engaged team because I'm committed to having my team be as successful as possible. I am personally committed to my leaders' growth and their individual prosperity.

When I have this kind of commitment to my team I am making a real difference in their lives, and this is priceless.

BTW – they will love you for being the one that leads the way. The one that gave them the biggest gift, the learning.

Watch a short video on "The How-to versus the Want-to"

https://qrco.de/bd6YHF

Chapter 13

Who Inspired You? Mentorship in the Hotel Business

Who inspired you? Who was the one person in your career for whom you would have done anything?

Be you for a moment and relive the experience you had when your career really took off. That place in your past when you were growing and learning your craft at a rapid rate. At that time you likely had someone in your world who was an inspiration, a bright light to follow. Some would call this person a mentor, a guide, an adviser— or maybe even a guru. This person took it upon themselves to help you find your way.

How exactly did they do that? What method or system did they use to help you?

"Show me a successful individual and I'll show you someone who had real positive influences in his or her life. I don't care what you do for a living—if you do it well, I'm sure there was someone cheering you on or showing the way. A mentor."

~ Denzel Washington

In the financial leader's world, this mentorship is a big deal—and it is also a great way to learn how to delegate. When I was in learning and growing mode, I had several mentors. Put simply, my mentors were people in the business who were ahead of me in knowledge, experience, and skills, so they could show me how to do something that I did not know how to do.

I've shared above the story of my boss assigning me—basically a rookie at the time—the task of preparing next year's budget for a 500-room hotel. You know it turned out well, and I learned a lot, but initially I thought my boss was crazy. I had never prepared a budget before.

At the time I had a good friend who was the Executive Chef in the same hotel. He was English and had a wicked sense of humor. We would often meet at the end of the workday in his office for a cold beer. On the day when I learned my boss was heading out on his big trip and leaving me all the work, including the budget, I told my friend over a beer that I was pretty sure I was being dumped on and taken advantage of.

At first he laughed and said, "I guess you're really screwed now!" But then he said something I will never forget. "Your bosses aren't stupid. They wouldn't leave this with you if you weren't ready."

I thought for a moment and realized that what he was saying was true. And furthermore, this was a *big* opportunity.

And it was. I learned so much, and it was phenomenal. If my boss hadn't left me with that "mess," I never would have learned what he taught me. And the process ultimately opened many doors for me and my career, all because my boss delegated to and believed in me.

The hotel business is an old-world business, you sit at the foot of the master and learn. You can't really go to school to learn this stuff, and even if you could, the real learning comes from doing. It's a people business—you're part of a team, and people can progress rapidly in hotels. Their growth trajectory is often fueled by having a mentor.

In my career I've had four or five really significant people who've helped me find my next job, either at the same hotel or in a different one. Manager, supervisor, executive—I, like most people in the hotel business, moved around a lot, and this was fueled by the whole process of mentorship.

Typically you'll get mentored by your boss, or even your boss' boss. One thing a mentee can do is learn to ask for help; people generally want to help, because someone helped them. It's a cultural thing in the hotel business. Ask questions, be hardworking and humble, know your strengths, go the extra mile, make sure things are looked after—including making your mentor look good—and be interested in what you're doing. It's not just a job you're doing—you're on a path.

Now, what if you want to *be* a good mentor? Have time for people. Take an interest in their career development. As a mentor you want to be looking to have a group of people to support. Not only is it a generous way to be—it's also true that they'll have your back and you'll be more successful in your own role. In other words, the mentoring process creates its own momentum.

Communicating, developing people, solving problems—this is what hospitality financial leadership is about. Good for mentor and mentee. If you take nothing else away from this book but the message of this chapter, it will have served its purpose.

Quick question: who are you believing in and who are you helping?

II

BUSINESS PRINCIPLES AND FINANCIAL STATEMENTS

This section is about the mechanics of the financials and the "why" behind them. The why is an important issue to examine because as adults we question why we need to do something, and especially "why" in a certain way. This section explores the universal principles of business and offers insights into how the financials work.

Chapter 14

The Basic Principles of Business

The accounting trade has a global language much like carpentry or plumbing. There are balance sheets, receivables, accruals and so on. And in general, there are universal rules as well—numbers, after all, are numbers wherever you go. The principles of accounting are exactly the same in the hotel business as they are in other businesses, the same for all the reaches of the globe. That's the good news.

These principles are the foundation that the business world relies on to ensure the relevance and meaning of financial information is the same. I will not go over all of them here, but in this chapter, I'll review some of the basic principles most relevant in the hotel world.

These principles connect everyday activities to the business of hotels so that you and other leaders (or up-and-coming leaders) can understand why we do what we do. This is powerful stuff, because there is a rhyme and a reason for everything we do. For many non-financial leaders, understanding this is the key to dropping their resistance and getting on board with the numbers.

Let's begin.

The Matching Principle and Accrual Versus Cash Accounting Systems

The number one principle that the entire hotel accrual accounting system is built on is the "matching principle." This principle dictates matching revenues with expenses to determine profitability within a given accounting period. It also means that the actual physical exchange of money and when it is received have no relevance to the financial (P&L) report. For example, if the hotel has a conference in June, expenses and revenue are matched for June, regardless of when the conference is paid for (say, in July). The matching principle is designed to give an accurate picture of revenues and expenses in a specific month or year. This principle is the juice that makes the month-end closing process fun. For instance, did everything get done in the month? Was the month close a clean one?

There are two different accounting systems to consider here, with one obvious pick for most hotels: the *accrual accounting system.* Only very small inns and bed and breakfasts use the *cash accounting system.* The difference between accrual and cash accounting systems has to do with when revenues and expenses are reported on a financial statement. The cash system calls for revenues and expenses to be realized (reported) when the money for a transaction changes hands. The accrual system realizes transactions when the related event occurs, and not when it's paid for. As noted above, if a conference takes place in June but isn't paid for until a later month, or is paid for in advance, it's included on the P&L for June. The accrual system allows greater flexibility in recording the complex workings of an organization (in this case, your hotel). It allows you to take into account all costs, such as payroll, that still need to be paid, or a large expense for an event that has happened but for which we haven't yet been paid by the customer.

Using the matching principle in conjunction with accrual accounting creates a more accurate picture of a hotel's profit or loss.

The hotel business is a retail business. Every day the property management system is closed off, as are the point-of-sale systems. Knowing *revenues* for a month is the starting point. Once you know this figure, you close the books and then determine the *costs* for the same period. This is where things get a little tricky. The monthly calendar was not designed to handle weekly or bi-weekly payroll, so we always need to accrue for the payroll missing until the end of the month, and also reverse the previous month's accrual. For example, generally June payroll is not paid out to employees until the first or second week of July, and this must be accounted for in June and then again in July. With expenses, be sure to accrue for items that were delivered or provided in, say, June, but for which no invoice was received in June.

This is an area where some people turn a blind eye to costs—what should be included (accrued)—with an eye only to making the end results look better than they are. This might mean "forgetting" to include a supplies order or unexpected expense. So it is an area that is vulnerable to manipulation, and if it's done improperly it can lead to significant issues. (Because of the importance of the "matching principle" I've dedicated the entire next chapter to it, so stay tuned.)

The Materiality Principle

Another very important principle, especially for hotels, is the materiality principle. What is "material"—important or relevant—to financial reporting, and how do we treat certain expenses? What is represented and what is omitted on balance sheets versus what is expensed when it is received, and why?

In the hotel industry we usually recognize some inventory as "material" and some as "immaterial." The difference lies in how we treat the items in question on a transaction basis. Here I will apply the materiality principle to inventory in the hotel trade where only "material assets" are recognized.

Tenderloin and toilet paper are two useful opposite examples of materiality in hotels. When you buy tenderloin, it is put into the inventory account on the balance sheet. This is done because it is valuable, and you sell filet mignon with a nice markup.

Toilet paper, however, is bought and immediately expensed. You bypass the balance sheet altogether and go directly to the profit and loss statement. You do this because toilet paper a) has a much lower value,

b) you do not sell it, and c) people are not likely to run off with it.

Tenderloin and toilet paper are treated differently because tenderloin is material and toilet paper is immaterial—in the hotel business.

The materiality principle helps maintain a level of efficiency when it comes to the number of items, we need to put on the balance sheet. If you noted everything that didn't really need to be there, the balance sheet would quickly become unwieldy.

The Business Entity Principle

This principle dictates that—unless a business is owned and run by a sole proprietor (as a bed and breakfast might be)—the assets of the business and the rights to *use* these assets are separate and distinct.

For example, if Henry Ford was still alive and CEO of the Ford Motor Company, the cars sitting on the factory's assembly line would not belong to him—they would (and did) belong to the shareholders of the Ford Motor Company.

In a hotel, the assets and liabilities of the company that owns the hotel are separate and maintained distinctly from the executives, principals, and employees of the business. The business principle also dictates that only transactions directly pertaining to the business are entered into the company's books.

From time to time, we hear in the news about executives or other employees who use certain company assets like jets to transport family on a holiday. This is rightly called out as an inappropriate use of company resources; the assets do not belong to the executives and, therefore, should not be used for their personal use. This is an area where a misuse of power can cause trouble for some people. (To reiterate this business entity principle applies to corporations where the ownership is separate from the individuals running the business.)

The Full Disclosure Principle

Numbers only give us part of a financial picture—more

specifically, they show what has happened financially to date.

For this reason, upcoming events that might have a material impact on the business need to be disclosed in writing for shareholders and stakeholders. Items like outstanding lawsuits, union matters, competition, environmental issues, pending changes in laws, insurance claims . . . anything that might have a negative or positive effect on future stability and earnings for the business must be disclosed.

These events are represented in business reporting as footnotes to the financial statements. In the case of the hotel, the monthly "Hotel Executive Commentary," "Property Report" or "Manager's Report" is the instrument for full disclosure. These reports are designed to include all of the items that *could* impact future earnings, as well as more detailed information, as needed, about what happened in the current reporting period. In addition, the commentary includes detailed information on market conditions and the business outlook going forward.

Basically, all investors and stakeholders need to know what is going to happen in the future—at least as much as possible—in order to make the best decisions possible for financial stability. A great example of this principle in most hotels is what we commonly call the "monthly commentary" or "owners report."

Watch a short video on the "Full Disclosure Principle"

https://qrco.de/bd6XBI

The Conservatism Principle

This principle states that the financials must fairly and

conservatively represent the business's current financial situation. The principle states to never overestimate revenues or underestimate expenses.

For example, a tenant might prepay rent for a year, but 100% of the revenue for that payment would not apply to the P&L that month; rather, only one-twelfth of it would. Another example is a cancellation fee. Sales contracts might include such an agreement with a client, and if the clause needed to be invoked, the revenue would not be recognized until it was paid.

On the flipside, *all* possible *negative* activity should be captured if it affects the period reported on. For instance, if a hotel has not yet received its electricity bill for the month and the data is needed to close the books, your estimate should err on the side of accruing the largest consumption to date, rather than the smallest.

Another example: if you are aware of pending litigation, explain now what might happen and give a liberal estimate of potential exposure and expense.

The essence of the conservatism principle is that information is reported in a way that 1) will allow management to minimize potential negative future financial impacts and 2) does not assume positive events will occur and alter the overall picture.

Assume the worst, don't hope for the best. It's not a good way to live your life, but it's a good way to create your financial statements.

The Objectivity Principle

The objectivity principle states that we must show proof of every financial transaction in the business. For every sale, there is a posting, a room charge, a restaurant slip, a bar bill, a banquet check. For every purchase, there is a purchase order, a receiving slip, an invoice and a check for payment. For every hour worked there is a schedule, a timecard and a payroll register.

In all, this principle states that evidence is needed to support everything. A manager cannot just make up transactions and record them; the backup must prove the entry. For example, the Director of Maintenance might want to accrue for an emergency plumbing repair that happened on the 30th of the month. There is no invoice, so a work order estimate or a purchase order that describes the problem, location, and estimated cost is required.

Watch this short video on the "Objectivity Principle"

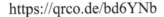

https://qrco.de/bd6YNb

The Consistency Principle

This principle simply indicates that it's important to follow a consistent process from one period to the other in the financial world. If the process needs to be changed, the necessary people are informed through the full disclosure principle.

Imagine, for example, that changes are needed in an inventory method. In the past, the "first in, first out" (FIFO) method was used to measure the value of beverage inventory. Then it was decided that the most efficient way to measure the value going forward was to use an average weighted cost. Disclosure of the change is required during the month the change was made so the stakeholders in the business see and understand the variance attributable to the change in accounting methods.

~

Enough on most accounting principles for now. Just remember that the hotel business, like all businesses, needs a structure. The structure needs principles that support the foundation. These processes allow for the consistent and relevant production of financial information.

Chapter 15

The Matching Principle

In this chapter, I am going to repeat part of the previous chapter but that's okay—because it is so important for you to completely grasp the idea. I tell my Hospitality Financial Leadership Workshop participants that the concept behind the matching principle is "the most important concept today." Why? When it comes to producing financial information, it's the cornerstone of understanding why we do almost everything the way we do it in the hotel business world. The profit and loss statement cannot exist and be in any way accurate without using the matching principle every step of the way. Grasp this and you are well on your way to understanding the other principles— and most importantly to putting these principles to work in your day-to-day hotel leadership role. This cannot be stressed enough, because the day-to-day operation of the hotel must be shaped knowing that all financial transactions are recorded in the month, for the month.

Some of you are probably thinking this is for the bean counters to chew on. Nothing could be further from reality. Being a financial leader means understanding and employing business principles. These principles are universal, and without them, you're like a plumber who doesn't understand why water flows the way it does. So read on and get your schtick together.

You may have endured the wrath of someone else when the financial statement came out in your hotel and you had expenses that month from a few months back. This was probably because someone else lost the invoice or failed to put it through to accounts payable. That is the matching principle getting abused! Here is what it's all about and how to use it properly.

The matching principle states: In order to have meaningful financial information we must match all revenues with their costs at the time the revenue was earned. That's the potentially confusing part: match all revenues with costs *regardless of when the money exchanges hands.*

That's right! We want to consistently match revenues with costs at the time the revenue is earned, regardless of when the money comes or goes. This is technically the definition of "accrual accounting," which is the polar opposite of "cash accounting." As noted in an earlier chapter, cash accounting realizes revenues and expenses when the money changes hands. You can compare the cash accounting system to the old shoe box. Money goes in the shoe box when people pay us, and money comes out when we pay for our costs. If there is money left in the shoe box that's our profit.

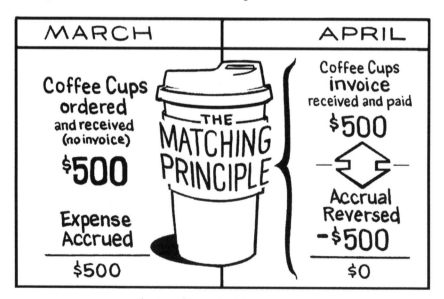

The Matching Principle:
- Recognizes revenue/costs in the month they happened
- Is flexible—it doesn't matter when the invoice is paid
- Ensures costs aren't recorded twice

The matching principle provides a much clearer and very precise picture of profitability because we don't need to take into consideration the timing of payments, either coming or going. It's not the case that the payments are not important. It's just not necessary to take the payments into consideration when we calculate our profit using the matching principle and accrual accounting.

So how does all of this relate to hotels? Here is an example from a client whom I recently helped transition from the cash basis to the accrual basis in his four hotels. He was confused because his monthly financial statements didn't always make sense. We discussed why the statements seemed too good to be true certain months—and downright awful in other months. He knew that he paid his people every two weeks, which means that every month you're only recording two pay periods. It also means that every six months you come across a month with three pay periods (that's just the way the calendar works). He also knew that annually, in June, he needed to pay the real estate taxes that covered the first half of the year and the next six months. Other items also made the statements wonky, like insurance, utilities, and benefits. Because of these kinds of things, he knew the statements were bogus; he had a timing problem. What he didn't know was how to fix it.

Introducing the two stars of this matching principle show: Mr. Prepaid and Mrs. Accrual. These might sound like ominous characters but, really, they are simple and straightforward. Mr. Prepaid acts to allow the insurance payment to be paid now and then have the cost split evenly into the next twelve months. This allows for a smooth ride of the profit and loss statement rather than having it all show up in one month, which is what would happen under the cash system. Mr. Prepaid only goes one way, pay it up front and then spread the cost evenly into the months that are covered. This is the matching principle in action.

Now let's look at Mrs. Accrual. She is a bit different in that she must go forward and backward. Anytime she goes one way she must eventually go the other way. Let's use payroll as an example. Every month I have two pay periods, and to properly match my revenues and expenses I need to accrue for the missing days. Well, guess what? Next month I need to do the same thing, but I also need to reverse the previous month's accrual, so I match that month's costs to the revenues. Accruals bring expenses into my month's statement before I have the actual invoice, or with the example of payroll, into my P&L before I pay people. In both expenses and payroll, I need to include everything that has been recognized this month regardless of whether I have paid for it yet or not. Once the accrual is booked (recorded), I'm now matched, and expenses incurred line up with the revenue earned. Once the accrual is recorded it's normally reversed the next month, because the actual invoice showed up and the payroll got paid.

I'm going to repeat myself again, but it's worth it because it is so important to understand this. The matching principle works on the idea that expenses and revenues all need to be included in each profit and loss reporting period, regardless of when the money for the revenue earned is collected or when the cash for the expenses (such as payroll) is paid out.

Get this into your DNA and make sure all your departments' expenses get booked properly or accrued each month. Those invoices and packing slips on your desk need to be sent down the hall so they are included in this month's results. Without the matching principle working smoothly and completely in your hotel, you will be in for a rough ride.

Watch this short video on the "Matching Principle"

https://qrco.de/bd6Z4V

Chapter 16

The Critical Importance of Accruals and Deferrals

A lot gets written about certain things in the hotel industry, but not so much about others. I am not saying it is simply a matter of blatant favoritism or anything like that, but it is not lost on me that certain items get the limelight. So to make up for that a little bit, in this chapter I am going to shine a light on two of the hotel team's third-line mainstays: accruals and deferrals. This pair keeps us on track month after month—and they need a little more respect.

Part of the respect for them comes from understanding their function and how important it is to the team's performance. Without this pair playing well, we are doomed. Each part of our operation needs to understand how they work and be sure to include them on each and every outing.

When we look into the business systems in our hotel, we want to see two things clearly every time.

We want to know how we are performing financially relative to the current budget and the previous year, both for the current month and for the year to date.

On top of that, we want to know where the improvements need to be made in order to get back on track, so we can make our numbers at the end of the year.

This pair of agents is like the defensive line in a football team. A good show means nothing gets by them; nothing gets through without proper authorization and credentials.

In order to produce an accurate picture of the business's financial performance, we need to match the revenues earned with the appropriate amount of costs, payroll and expenses—that's the matching principle again. There is no way to accomplish this without the use of accruals and deferrals. They make the show work, and they do so in a spectacular fashion without even so much as a complaint or request for attention—as long as YOU don't forget to include them.

If we try and run the financial system without the full complement of accruals and deferrals, we may look like we're on top of the situation. But, alas, only to learn that it is short-lived, and the lack of a critical process shows up next month and effects all subsequent periods of the game.

Accruals sometimes get a bad rap. When we forget to include them, they make their presence known, although you may not hear from them immediately. We try and round them all up every month and if we forget one or two there is likely hell to pay. That is why they get a bad rap because they point out the offending department and manager with the cry of a spoiled victory. You do not want to be the one who forgot their accruals! This simply means you let down your team.

Deferrals, on the other hand, seemingly can save the day. When it appears the game is lost, the quiet and unassuming linebacker delivers a one-two punch and brings much relief to the team's efforts. Deferring expenses to future periods with a legitimate match to the upcoming revenues is a sweet sound indeed.

Accruals and deferrals are on the same line – let's call it the adjustment line – but they play different positions. Accruals bring expenses into the current period and they are always promptly and completely reversed in the following period. In and out just like that. Here one month and gone the next. Deferrals have a longer, more purpose-filled role. A deferral can play a full twelve months and contribute to each performance, unlike the accrual that always comes and goes. A great example is the insurance bill.

You can look at an accrual like it is a substitution for a real player. We substitute the accrual when we do not yet have the real thing. Usually, it is the invoice that is missing. You can look at the deferral like it is being sliced up into bite-sized pieces so we can digest it smoothly. We know what it feels like if we consume too much.

Well, there you have it. Realizing these two play pivotal roles in our financial performance is key to a successful campaign. Always bring them both completely and fully to every game and show them the respect they deserve, because without them you are not going to be successful.

Watch this short video on "Accruals and Deferrals"

https://qrco.de/bd74qQ

Chapter 17

Hotel Current Assets

I am going to explore what is unique about hospitality assets and how we record and use them. In this chapter I am only going to talk about current assets.

An asset is something you have paid for or earned previously that can be used to generate more income. That is the critical test: Can you use this item to make more money, to create more economic activity?

Items like tenderloin, tequila, and the guest and city ledgers (the money you receive from paying guests) are all good examples of things you can use to make more money. You prepare the tenderloin and tequila and sell it for four to six times what you paid for it. You can use guest and city ledgers once they are collected to buy more tenderloin and tequila. And on it goes.

An asset is part of the balance sheet, and it can travel over to the profit and loss statement as an expense or cost of goods sold. In hospitality, current assets typically consist of cash, accounts receivable, inventory and prepaids. That's pretty much it for a hotel. Of course, there are others, but on a hotel balance sheet, you will always find these four. In other industries, current assets will be made up of what is unique to that business. If the business is making cars, assets probably include cash, steel, wire, tires. If selling clothes, current assets might include cash, sweaters, and jeans. Each different industry is unique.

One thing you will not see recorded in your assets is people. We always say that people are our number one asset in the hotel business. Brand slogans and company cultures are built on this steadfast ideal. And in most cases, it's true that our people are our most valuable asset. However, we do not account for this value on our balance sheet.

A Note on Guest Ledgers and City Ledgers

Guest ledgers and city ledgers often trip people up when looking at assets. Let's demystify them.

The word "ledger" simply means a list. The guest ledger is the value of the accounts in-house for all our current guests, their rooms, taxes, restaurant charges, parking, and so on. It is a total of what each one owes the hotel while in-house.

Imagine, if you will, that we line up all our guests in the lobby. Each one owes us money, and the sum of all the guest accounts is the total guest ledger. And as pointed out above, you can use this money to make more money.

The city ledger is the value of all the credit arrangements and the resulting billings that the guests and groups have made with the hotel. The city ledger is unique to the hotel service world. We extend our guests credit! Can you imagine your airline giving you a master account?

Never. So why do we extend credit like we do with our guests? The answer is twofold. One, we have always done this. In our business, the practice of extending credit goes way back to a time even before currency. The second more obvious reason is that our competition does this, too. This means we also need to give credit, or we risk losing a competitive edge. Now that I think about it, the whole credit world in hotels is ripe for some disruption!

The Life Cycle of an Asset

Current assets live on the balance sheet, and they serve one purpose: to fuel the profit and loss statement. If we take the tenderloin example again, start at the beginning and go through its life cycle, it looks like this:

The owner invests his money and adds cash to the business as a current asset. The cash is used to buy tenderloin. The tenderloin is used to sell filet mignon and the asset leaves the balance sheet and travels to the profit and loss statement as the cost of goods. Cost of goods is an expense and, at the same time, it creates income and corresponding payment for the four to six times sale price. Now there is more cash to buy more tenderloin and toilet paper, and on it goes.

You can look at any current asset in the same light. They do not all directly get sold like the tenderloin, but they all fuel the profit and loss statement and eventually find their way there.

Understanding current assets in the hotel business is manageable for anyone who is a department head or who aspires to be one. Do not get fooled into thinking it is a big, complicated dance. Remember the three principles: cost, materiality, and consistency. The next time your hotel financial statement lands on your desk or in your mail, go see your friendly financial professional and review the current assets:

- Which ones do you have in your hotel?
- How does your hotel treat certain items?
- Which items are put on the balance sheet and which items are expensed?
- What unique current assets does your hotel have?

Expand your understanding a step at a time.

Watch a short video on "Hotel Assets"

https://qrco.de/bd6XKi

Chapter 18

Liabilities

When I do financial leadership workshops with hotel teams, we often talk about two key liabilities I know they all have: vacation and wages.

Every employee knows how many vacation days they've got, and also how much money is owed to them in wages. In business terms, these are liabilities for the hotel. The individual employee thinks vacation pay is a good thing. And it is—for them. For the employer, it is anything but good, because they need to pay the employee when he or she isn't there.

Vacation pay is an excellent example with which to illustrate the three-part test we'll always need to use to determine our business liabilities.

Liability Test – Part One: The Liability Has Already Occurred

Liabilities need to have already occurred. Like the vacation pay we all have, it was earned yesterday, last week, last month, last year. Therefore, it already happened. Your employer has been keeping track of your earnings. And every pay period they squirrel away a little extra expense for your upcoming holiday. This way they match the expense for your vacation when you earn it, not when you take it. Note here they squirrel away the expense in the form of a liability, not the cash.

Liability Test – Part Two: The Liability Is the Responsibility of the Hotel

All liabilities impose a duty or responsibility. Vacation pay fits this bill. Wages owed to an employee are another great example. There is no question that your employer owes you wages you already earned. It is part of the social contract between you and your boss. They are on the hook to pay you.

Liability Test – Part Three: The Liability Is Unavoidable

With all liabilities, there is no room for avoidance. If your boss tried to cheat you out of your vacation pay or wages earned, they would face the local labor board or some other government body that would make sure you got paid.

~

So, to summarize: A liability has already happened, it's an obligation, and there is no way to avoid it.

Other liabilities that you'll find on any hotel balance sheet include:

- Accounts Payable – This is the outstanding list of vendors' invoices that need to be paid for goods and services the hotel has already received.

- Sales Tax Payable – This is the sales tax for rooms and food and beverage that the hotel has collected from prior sales. It is typically collected for one month, then paid to the local or state/provincial government. The hotel has already collected the tax, and it is obligated to remit the money. Failure to do so will land you in a pile of dung. (Even being a day late can be extremely expensive; I know this from firsthand experience.)

- Advance Deposits – This is a tricky one, because we naturally think of a deposit as a good thing. Not so fast. Let's look at the three-part test. It already happened (the deposit was paid), and in most cases if the client cancels in the appropriate amount of time we need to refund the deposit. Advance deposits have an important characteristic, too, in the sense that the deposit is a non-event for the profit and loss statement; we have not yet earned the income. We only get to book the revenue for the deposit when the guest actually comes and stays a night or has their event. Only then do we recognize the revenue.

- Accruals: A final example is a general one. Whenever you see the word "accrued" in front of the title of a balance sheet account, you can bet your paycheck that it is a liability. Accrued utilities, accrued vacations, accrued salaries, accrued bonuses, accrued worker's compensation—these are all liabilities, because they clearly pass the three-way test. They've already occurred, they impose an obligation on the budget, and you can't avoid them.

Watch a short video on "Liabilities"

https://qrco.de/bd6Wye

Chapter 19

How to Read the Hotel Financial Statements and the Link

The first thing you need to know about reading a hotel financial statement is that there are two different "primary" statements you'll want to get comfortable with:

1. The income statement (most people call it the P&L or "Profit and Loss" statement).

2. The balance sheet

Now you might be thinking that balance sheets are for the accounting types, as they're most certainly complicated. Nothing could be further from the truth. In this chapter we'll discuss them, and I'll share a secret about the balance sheet and its relationship to the P&L.

One thing to always keep in mind is something many miss: in hospitality we do what we do the way we do it because of the book.

The *Uniform System of Accounts for the Lodging Industry* lays out in excruciating detail the standards for our industry. (Always get the latest version of this essential book.)

The USALI is a great resource for defining what goes where and for standardizing formats for the hotel financial statement, but it does not include several key aspects—like flow thru and productivity reporting—which are incredibly powerful and useful tools. In any case, if you are serious about hotel financial knowledge, I highly recommend you get yourself a copy.

More on "you Sally" (USALI) in the next chapter.

Income / Profit and Loss Statement

First, let's be clear: hotel income statements are free-form items and are not all created equal. What I mean is that each business is free to set them up as they see fit. That said, one characteristic of hotel statements that are set up using USALI have is that they are all set up by department.

They usually go in the following order:

- Rooms department
- Food and Beverage department
- Minor operating departments, such as: golf, spa, telephone, and laundry.

These departments are called "operating departments" because they all generate income.

Next come the non-operating departments, which include:

- Administration and general
- Sales and marketing
- Maintenance & energy

These departments are called "non-operating" because they do not generate any income. I know some of you think the sales department makes money—but not so fast. Sales books business, but the rooms department generates the income when the guest actually stays in the hotel.

Inside each department you will see the same layout:

- Income
- Cost of sales (if required)

- Payroll and benefits
- Expenses

The Summary Statement

A good summary P&L is probably the most read and highly anticipated financial statement in any hotel.

The P&L usually starts with a summary or overall report, and this is where you will want to start your review. Here you should find total revenues for all hotel activities and the total costs, leading you to the gross operating profit and net operating profit lines. The statement is usually laid out so you can see the results of the month compared to the budget and/or forecast for that same month, as well as a comparison to the previous year's figures. In addition to the month's numbers, you will want to see the accumulated year-to-date (YTD) results, normally to the right of the monthly numbers.

In the YTD you want to see the accumulated result. Let's say you're looking at November in the current year. You will want to look at:

- Accumulated budget values up until November
- Accumulated YTD for the previous year up until November (of the previous year)

Always compare like periods of time in the P&L, as well as the previous year, to the actual monthly and YTD amounts.

Individual Department Statements

Next, moving beyond the summary statement, you will find the balance of the income statement laid out by department in the same order you see at the top level. Each of these departmental statements will have totals for revenue, cost of sales (food and beverage, spa, telephone), payroll and expense that need to tie back to the summary statement.

Once people make this connection it all comes together rather quickly. What you may have previously thought was a complicated and confusing report becomes far more straightforward.

Why Is the P&L so Important?

The P&L (income statement) is really the most interesting statement because it shows you how you are doing related to profit or loss for a given period of time. It is a snapshot of what revenues and costs are for the period you're looking at. If you are looking at the June statement and it's December, it really isn't relevant. The income statement tells how you are doing financially regarding the operating profit. It is how you keep score relative to the budget (the promise) and last year. You can clearly see these comparisons for the most current month and year-to-date.

The P&L allows you to see where operations are successful and where they're facing challenges. This is pivotal; in fact, it's really the main purpose of the income statement.

How can you improve? Is payroll too high? Are expenses out of control? Are revenues falling short of the budget? How much more payroll than last year? It all comes out on the income statement. Like a report card and a wake-up call to pull up your socks and your marks too. This is where the income statement transcends the black and white piece of paper and becomes the vehicle for change and ideas. Get your team involved and change the way you manage.

That's what's possible using financial leadership.

The Balance Sheet

The second most common statement you want to be comfortable reviewing every month is the balance sheet. The balance sheet tests the fundamental accounting equation. The equation states that:

$$\text{assets} = \text{liabilities} + \text{equity}$$

Most people get quiet here because it sounds like we're talking mumbo jumbo.[2] But really, this concept is very easy to grasp, and once you get it, you'll see the world of finance in a completely different light. What's more, it's like riding a bike—once it clicks you won't ever go back to struggling to get it.

When I teach my students this concept in my workshops, they often comment that they had no idea it was so simple.

I liken the explanation of the fundamental accounting equation to the ownership value relationship of a house. You—along with the bank—own the house. In this example, the house has a market value of $500,000 and you have a mortgage of $350,000 on the house through the bank. You subtract your mortgage from the value of the house, and that's your share. Or, in accounting terms, your owner's equity is:

$$\$500,000 \text{ (assets)} - \$350,000 \text{ (liabilities)} = \$150,000 \text{ (equity)}$$

This basic concept is exactly the same as the balance sheet mechanics. It is the "fundamental accounting equation."

You can run the most complicated business in the world and everything will still boil down to the same concept:

$$\text{assets} = \text{liabilities} + \text{equity}$$

In the example of the house, it's clear that the $150,000 is yours. In business, the assets minus the liabilities is what the owner is entitled to—their equity.

It is important to remember that the equity can also be a negative. Using the example of the house, and given the financial crisis of 2008, you know houses can end up with bigger mortgages than their value. In a business, you want to have a healthy asset-to-liability ratio, but

---

[2] For more discussion on this topic you can also revisit Chapter 7, "She Said She Was Born Without the Financial Gene."

this is not always the case. So, knowing this simple equation you can now test the health of the business by examining the values of total assets and liabilities.

The quality of those assets in a hotel should be relatively easy to measure. Cash, receivables, inventory, prepaid expenses . . . You use these items to make money, hence they are assets.

The liabilities are all the commitments you have that you must honor. Vendors to pay, deposits for future guests, taxes collected that need to be paid, employee wages, vacations to honor . . .

In simplistic terms, you have the good stuff (the assets) minus the bad stuff (the bills you need to pay). The difference is the equity.

The Link

The link between the P&L statement and the balance sheet is an important and powerful concept.

When you make a profit or have a loss in your business, you can see the bottom-line number in the year-to-date column on the income statement, usually called the net profit, or net operating profit, NOP.

What you can also see is that it is the same number on the balance sheet when you look at the current year's retained income or earnings line in the equity section.

The other line, called "retained income from prior periods," represents the accumulated profits and losses since the business was created. This is the link between the current year's profit performance and the lifetime of the business's accumulated profit and/or loss results.

The business and its balance sheet only get created when it is bought/sold. A new set of books is created, and you start everything from the purchase price values. Everything from that point forward moves from the income statement each month to the balance sheet, and its accumulated profit or loss is found in the equity.

$$\text{assets} = \text{liabilities} + \text{equity}$$

See? Not so difficult.

Watch a short video on the "Two Principal Statements and the Link"

https://qrco.de/bd6XMy

Chapter 20

A Bit About You Sally (USALI)

We've mentioned USALI a few times already, but since this is such an important reference in the hotel industry, I wanted to devote a brief chapter to the topic.

By someone's estimate there are roughly one million hotels in the world. I take it that that number includes all the different kinds of hotels, from small inns and hostels all the way up to your full-service, multi-outlet, mega-hotel operations. For simple math I am going to estimate that half of this number of hotels fall into the small inns and hostels, and that leaves 500,000 of what I'm going to call "real" hotels.

Of those 500,000 I am willing to bet that 50% do not know about or use "You Sally." If we ramp that number up by multiplying the 250,000 real hotels by the average number of department managers, GMs and owners, let's say ten per property, we have roughly 2.5 million hotel management people that do not know about "You Sally" or "USALI"—the *Uniform System of Accounts for the Lodging Industry.*

I think it is time that everyone in our industry who considers themselves a real hotelier take up the cause and bring Sally into their world. Sally is unique, and a gift that we can all benefit from. She not only has a lot of experience, she is also recognized around the world by brands, management companies, franchisors, banks and consultants as the authority when it comes to how you dress your hotel financials.

USALI has been around for almost a hundred years. She started out as a guidebook for the Hotel Accountants Association of New York City in the late 1920s. Since then she has been adopted by the American Hotel Association, and most recently by the association Hospitality Financial and Technology Professionals, or perhaps better known as HFTP.

She is the bible for the financial standards in the hotel industry, providing a solid and usable framework for our industry to follow when it comes to how we present financial information.

Chapter 21

Profit and Loss Statement Features

For some readers this may admittedly be a more complex chapter, though I hope it's helpful in giving an overview of several "advanced" features of the P&L. Simply having a sense that these options exist can serve you down the road.

Do your hotel financial statements give you the information you need to effectively run your business? Are you able to see if your profits are where they should be in an enhanced, top-line statement? Do your statements measure flow thru? Do you record your room's business by proper segments (i.e., customer types: Leisure, Corporate, etc.) and track the rooms occupied, rate and revenue in each segment? Do you record customers served in F&B and do you separate meal periods? Do you record liquor, beer, wine, and mineral sales on your financials separately? Do you measure labor productivity in your financials? Do you record hours of work in your financials? Do you have payroll segmented by management and hourly classifications? Do you have a separate supplemental payroll and benefits statement? Do you track arrivals and departures?

Most statements I see do not have most of these critical elements. They're lacking these incredibly effective items that can easily be added. Most people use the standard format as outlined in the Uniform System of Accounts for the Lodging Industry. This is great; however, you have the ability to produce an enhanced statement with just a little more detail added that will greatly assist you in effectively managing your business.

How would these elements add insight and value to your business?

Let's explore this. I've seen hotel financial statements in at least a hundred different formats (just do a quick Google search for "hotel financial statements"). In this chapter I'm going to lay out my version of what has worked best for me.

Top-Line Property Operating Statement Showing Divisional Results in a Summary Format

This simple and incredibly effective presentation is almost always absent. Hotels will have what they think is a top-line summary but it is usually not properly set up.

A proper and useful top-line statement will have total hotel revenue first. The statement has the current month on the left and it is compared to budget/forecast and last year, descriptions down the center and actual year-to-date on the right followed by budget YTD and YTD last year.

Next the rooms section: total room revenues, total payroll, total other expense.

Next is total rooms expenses and, finally, rooms profit. Five lines total. Beside every number is the percentage, so 100% for the revenue, 15% for the payroll and 10% for the expenses, 25% for the total expense and 75% for rooms profit. Right off the bat, you see what matters and we see the same percentages in the budget and last year columns.

Next the total F&B section with total food revenue, total beverage revenue, total other F&B revenue, and then total F&B revenue. Next is food cost, then beverage cost, and if applicable other costs of sales, then the total cost of sales. Next, its total F&B payroll followed by F&B expenses, total F&B departmental expenses, and then total F&B profit, 11 lines.

Again, and always, we see percentages within the department.

What percent of total F&B sales are beverages? What's my food cost percent this month compared to the budget and last year? It's all here.

Next are the same totals for all minor operating departments (MOD), with the cost of sales, payroll and expense totals, then MOD profit.

The next line is other income not including store rents.

This brings us to the "gross operating income" line (GOI), which equals all profits from all operating departments, a critical navel-gaze in your hotel.

The next part is for non-operating departments. We start with A and G: total payroll, total expenses, then total A and G, 3 lines. Then it is sales and marketing then POMEC or as some like to call it, maintenance, and it has an extra line for total utilities. The next line is total non-operating department costs, the sum of the three departments above. In most hotels, this is the protruding waistline and it's critical to see it clearly.

The last line before GOP is store rents and it is only for pure retail rent. If you run your own shop, it's an MOD. The GOP line is critical in that it is the manager's number, everything above this line is within his or her control, everything below the line is an owner's number.

Below GOP we want to see management fees. Then it is insurance, property taxes, leasing costs, debt or other financing costs, and lastly depreciation and reserve for F F and E. Below this, you will want to layout the occupancy, rate, and REVPAR totals. Next, it's a F&B customer (covers) summary and average spend, and last, it's a payroll and EFTE summary. If set up properly all of this can be captured in two pages.

For most executives, you should be able to get 95% of what you need to see to manage your business from this report. From this greatly enhanced report, you will know where you need to spend your time working on your operation.

Flow Thru

It's great to see revenues and profits. But how much of my additional revenue flows to the profit line, or better still, when revenues are declining, how much profit did we preserve? Each area as outlined above can be set up to highlight the flow thru to the prior period for the month and YTD as well as the flow to the budget and forecast.

An incredibly valuable tool is to be able to see the rooms' flow thru, F&B flow, MOD flow, and NOD flow. With these numbers laid out, you can very quickly see where your revenues are being eaten and how much profit made it thru. Without a flow thru statement in your monthly financials, you are left to look through the fog of numbers. With the proper flow thru statement and some flow thru standards, you are quickly seeing your operations and what's working and not.

We have a full chapter dedicated to flow thru coming up.

Rooms Segmentation

Knowing who your customers are is critical to your ongoing marketing efforts, and always striving to be as diversified as possible with segments is critical to weathering any upcoming economic storm. For display purposes, you want to lay things out so you can see the room revenue for the segment; the number of rooms sold, the rate and how many points of real occupancy this segment produced. We want to track the segments that are relevant to our hotel. At the very least you're probably going to want to see:

- Transient full
- Transient discount
- Packages
- Internet OTA
- Corporate
- Government

- Corporate meeting
- Convention
- FITs

The segmentation is the DNA for your hotel and not knowing where your business comes from in detail is obviously not good. With the proper layout, we will see what the different segments bring you, and with a little work we can line up the distribution costs, payment costs and additional spend from each broad segment giving us great insight into the profitability of each individual segment.

Knowing the segment with the highest room rate is one thing; however, knowing the different costs and spend is also critical. The group rate might be lower than the transient, but stop and look at the distribution costs on each side. The transient almost always comes with some commission, they arrive sporadically, they can make a mess, some spend in F&B maybe and then they pay their account with a credit card. On the flip side, the group arrives en masse, they usually send a rooming list or another non-commissionable method. They tend to move together in the hotel: meals, receptions and best of all they usually pay by check—especially if I make this part of the sales process, to nail down the payment method. With a big group, this can be several thousands of dollars. Understanding segmentation is critical.

Customer Covers

Do you record F&B customer statistics by meal periods, beverage sales by type?

Recording F&B customers is essential to measuring pricing strategies and it is the first half of getting productivity statistics working for you. Breaking your food sales down into meal periods is necessary to be able to track business volumes throughout the day in your outlets. Having proper meal periods with the sales, the number of customers, and average customer for each period compared to budget and last year for this month and year-to-date is what you need to manage your F&B world. Couple this with beverage sales broken down by liquor, beer, wine and minerals.

Understanding the makeup of the meal periods and average prices is important because we need to know where we are making our revenue and what produces the highest profit.

The typical periods you should be measuring in your full-service hotel are breakfast, lunch, dinner, reception and coffee breaks. It's amazing what you can see when these numbers are broken out this way, especially when we can see what it takes to put together a dinner versus breakfast, or a coffee break versus lunch. I ask this question a lot in my seminars: "Where do we make the most money in selling food in your hotel?" The immediate answers are usually dinner, heck, look at the large volume of sales and average customer spend. But then cooler heads prevail and it is almost always unanimous that breakfast is the most profitable and coffee the highest margin. Why breakfast? Look at the labor we need in front and especially behind the scenes for dinner and the mise en place, and you quickly and often conclude that breakfast, especially in banquets, is king.

With beverage sales, we want to see these broken out and we want to be able to track the cost of sales on each. Where do we make the most money in the beverage trade? Not the most sales but the highest profit. In America, it is hands down: liquor. With liquor costs, less than 10% most of the time we love hosted bars and receptions. Wine on the other hand has a nice price but costs are usually 30% or higher. What are you telling the sellers in your conference and catering departments to sell?

Measuring Productivity on Your Financial Statements

The only truly effective way to measure labor productivity in the hotel business is by expressing the productivity in hours per room occupied in the rooms division, hours per customer cover served in the F&B division and EFTEs per 100 rooms available in the non-operating departments. We have a full chapter coming up in the next section on EFTEs and productivity.

Separate Schedules for Supplemental Payroll and Payroll Benefits

Having these two additional costs separated and summarized on a separate schedule is both very handy and useful. These costs are usually allocated to each department using hours worked or some other allocation basis. To be able to see them in total is critical. Without the totals, we don't know the overall picture relative to budget and last year. We have a chapter dedicated to this in the next section.

Tracking Arrivals and Departures and Average Guests Per Stay

I once had a hotel in my region that had an average length of stay of 13 days. Needless to say, this hotel was unique. On the other side of that, I also know an airport hotel that has an average stay of less than 1 day. This statistic allows us to measure the amount of activity for the bell desk and front desk as well as the demand on the room attendants as stay overs are easier to clean than departures. Stay overs mean no additional work for the front desk, door or bell desk. The average length of stay also can point to early or delayed capital needs for everything from the room renovation to the carpets and other operating equipment. A general rule of thumb in rooms is the higher the average length of stay the better the labor productivity should be. This statistic is calculated by dividing the number of rooms occupied by the arrivals. Finally, we're wanting to measure and see the average number of guests per stay. We can achieve this by recording the number of guests in the room and dividing the aggregate of these by the total number of rooms sold. This is particularly useful for measuring F&B capture and it also points to linen and amenity consumption. Typically, the lower the number of guests the lower the laundry and amenity costs per room occupied.

Watch a short video on the "Top 10 Financial Statement Attributes"

https://qrco.de/bd6eBI

Chapter 22

Share the Financials in Your Hotel or NOT

Let's shift gears from the technical details and remind ourselves of an important theme of this book: making the numbers—the third pillar, along with Guest Service and Colleague Engagement—relevant and accessible to everyone. Your leadership in this area can make all the difference.

In your hotel, you either share the financials with your leaders—the department managers—or you don't.

If you don't share, you're wondering what your management team thinks about the money and how much of it goes to you and the owner.

You may (naively) think no one needs to know about the finances in your hotel. You tell yourself it's none of their business. Money stats are top secret and released only on a need-to-know basis.

In fact, you're pretty sure your team would judge you and your results—and if they knew the financial figures, this would be very easy for them to do. Maybe that reason alone is a good rationale for keeping things under your hat.

Of course, if you already share the financial statements, you know the power it unleashes with your team and the results it helps to create.

Let's explore the relationship we have with the money and how we can get the financials out of the closet.

If you're in the camp that says, "We don't share"—why is that? What's holding you back? Is there really a policy in your company that states the sharing of financial information is prohibited?

I'm pretty sure places that make rules like that are few and far between.

More likely you're encountering a "that's-just-the-way-it-is" problem. Someone will say, "That's just what we do," "We've always done it this way." Or maybe it's a variation on "The last guy or gal didn't share either."

I'm willing to bet that most of you reading this could make the decision to share the financials with your department managers, especially if you had a sense as to what would be accomplished if you did. Isn't that an exciting prospect? Changing the way you manage and introducing a new process to generate a different result?

The financial statements serve two purposes in our business. One, they are the means by which we keep score in the game we call the hotel business. Whether or not your business is prospering is revealed by the numbers in your statements. A quick look by someone who knows how to read the statement will reveal the truth. I know many hoteliers don't share because they're embarrassed by the lack of prosperity they're experiencing. The very thought of sharing this with their managers is too much to take.

In our culture money has immense power. If we allow this power to dominate our actions, we're giving into an unhealthy fear, one that holds us down and keeps us from wrapping our arms around our business and getting the results we know are possible.

"People will think I'm incompetent," is one of those fears. I often hear it's the owner who doesn't want the financials distributed. This might be justified by saying the managers and department leaders need to look after the guests and their colleagues, not worry about the money.

No matter what the excuse or reason, there's one key question to ask: "Do you think you could achieve a better financial result if your leaders and managers knew what was happening financially?"

When I ask this question, the inevitable answer—sometimes accompanied by a deer-in-the-headlights stare—is, "Yes, but . . ."

I recommend you stop at "Yes."

In addition to keeping everyone aware of where you're at financially, the second purpose for involving your department managers in the financial statements is to help you to create plans and actions to improve everyone's results. Really this is the BIGGEST and HIGHEST purpose financial statements can serve in your business.

- How am I doing?
- What's the score?
- What can I do to improve?

Your financials point the way forward. If you're doing something well, you know to keep doing it, and maybe even do it better. If you're doing something wrong, the financials will help you pick that out.

If we don't know what's wrong with a patient, prescribing a proper cure is beyond anyone's ability. A close review of your financial statements will reveal exactly what's wrong with your business, if anything, and how to possibly cure it.

Now, when we look at ways to improve, we naturally want the maximum buy-in from our managers and leaders to help pull it off. So, ask yourself, how can you get your managers to really own their actions going forward. How can you get your team as engaged as possible financially?

Share the financials.

Involve them in the formulation of the profit improvement plans. The numbers will help everyone isolate what's working and what's not, and everyone can be in on the process.

This really is not a new or leading-edge strategy. It's as old as the hills. If you want buy-in and accountability from your people, it will NEVER HAPPEN if you don't share the financials. Your managers won't have the information they need to step up to the plate and participate.

Why not?

Because you can't expect someone to create results that are better than their current ones if they don't know what the initial results are and what the new ones should look like.

You're leaving them adrift at sea without any way to navigate and no idea of where to go.

Your leaders want to make a difference in their lives, at work and at home. All of us have a basic human need to make a difference. Of course, your managers want to have a greater impact on your business results. They want to know the score, the scoop. They want their seat at the captain's table. They want to be on the inside track.

And they want you to treat them like adults. Sharing the financial results and asking for their participation is an incredibly powerful gesture. It also needs to be done properly, with just the right amount of humility and vulnerability. Yes, vulnerability. When you share your results, you're opening up a part of yourself and your side of the business that they know is sensitive and personal. When you share your financial results, you create equity with your leaders. Manage this process carefully and you can turn your financial world around.

One more thing, which we've been stressing a lot so far in this book. Financial leadership skills are incredibly valuable assets for your managers to create. With these skills, they are highly marketable in our industry. And these skills cannot be picked up at school or from a textbook. The only place you can learn how to manage the Profit and Loss statement in your department is on the job.

And if you're a financial leader, you have capacity and capability to create these financial leadership skills within your managers. Do you remember what it was like when you were younger and someone took you under his or her wing, guided and mentored you? You have this same opportunity to create that priceless relationship with your managers. Do this for them and they'll move mountains for you and your business.

And if you are a departmental manager or someone in the business who wants to understand the numbers and see how the pieces of the financial picture fit together, approach the financial leaders in your hotel and start learning.

Chapter 23

The Paper Can't Talk

In the hotel business, we have three equal pillars: the guest, the colleague, and the money.

This third pillar, money, needs a proper voice. A voice that speaks to the leadership necessary to create positive progressive management. But if the paper is going to have a voice, we want to make sure it's the proper one. We want it to be a voice that gives equity to all our constituents.

Far too often, the voice of the money is scary, stingy, or downright mean. You're probably thinking that the Director of Finance sure makes enough noise about the numbers and schedules for month-end and the variances to forecast. He or she is very vocal at the department head meetings, always saying what's wrong, what's late, what didn't work. You're also thinking that the Owner and Asset Manager are always getting the hotel to cut back, all to drive the bottom line.

In short, the financial voice in most hotels is LOUD, and it's almost always negative.

There's never enough. Someone's always wanting more. There's an endless need to be fed. This is what happens to the voice of money if we don't address the way in which we craft, package, and deliver the money message.

What if the voice of the money received the same respect and understanding that the voice of the guest has? Or the voice of the colleague?

It's possible to create the kind of environment in which this is the case. The key is understanding. It's important to understand why the money needs a special voice and why it gets a bad rap if we don't give it one.

Money usually gets a bad reputation for three reasons.

One, money is a powerful part of our society's fabric. If you don't have money or you think you need more, that's a powerful negative force, a drain on your energy and your business's. There's a feeling that if you run out of money, it's all over.

Two, lack of money is usually used to shame people. If you don't have enough, surely there's something you're missing, something you're not doing. You're not keeping up.

Third, as part of our culture, the very subject of money is still largely taboo. Certainly, we don't typically have open conversations about where we're at with it.

So, if we want to have a positive relationship with the money in our hotel, we need to get it out of the dark closet and place it front and center. We need to give the money a fair, friendly and equitable voice. After all, money is just a way to measure and exchange value in our world.

To give the money that kind of voice requires adopting certain strategies and practices. The first is open access to financial information. Budgets, forecasts, and actual results are all shared in your hotel. Managers and leaders at all levels are part of the creation of the budget and forecast, and they share updates regularly with their departments and colleagues. Success is celebrated, and rewards for financial gains are shared.

The sharing part is critical, though it might mean different things in different businesses and relationships. It could be profit sharing, bonuses, or celebrations. It really doesn't matter as long as you're sharing the prosperity. Then, in times of constraint when revenues decline, we have a leg to stand on with our teams. For example, no one likes it when expenses and staffing need to be adjusted downward to reflect decreased revenue. But an engaged workforce that knows what the score is will be much more willing to do their part if they already feel like they're part of a team. This is the only way to break out of the cycle that would otherwise have the money be the instrument that victimizes the workforce—right when we need them on board more than ever.

We can't have our cake and eat it too. That is, if we expect people to share in the hard times, we should share the times of bounty with them as well.

The core of our industry is hospitality. Usually, we only think of that in terms of our guests. But hospitality is equally important when it comes to our colleagues. If we truly desire a team that actively looks after our guests, then surely the executive, the leadership, the owner, the money—all of these things can also be looking after our colleagues. This means in part that the voice of money in our culture is one of caring and fairness.

Giving the money this kind of voice in your hotel creates an incredibly engaged team in your business, a team that respects you because of your openness. This team lifts your business up with many hands.

Just remember whatever path you choose, the voice of the money will be heard. It can be kind and just or feared.

It's up to you to decide what it will say.

Watch a short video on "The Paper Can't Talk"

https://qrco.de/bd6YkU

SCAN ME

Chapter 24

Financial Statement Analysis and Your Hotel Career

If you Google the words "financial statement analysis," you will get a long list of definitions, like this one by Wikipedia:

"Financial statement analysis (or financial analysis) is the process of reviewing and analyzing a company's financial statements to make better economic decisions. These statements include the income statement, balance sheet, statement of cash flows, and a statement of changes in equity. Financial statement analysis is a method or process involving specific techniques for evaluating risks, performance, financial health, and future prospects of an organization."[3]

What it will mean to you as a leader in the hospitality business is exactly the same and then some.

"What information can I get from my monthly P&L to understand my business and make better decisions?" and "What's going on in my business?" The latter is the better, more applicable, piece for an operations manager who has a healthy sense of curiosity and a leader who wants to make a difference.

Anyone can look at the statement and see that one number is

---

[3] Wikimedia Foundation. (2021, December 10). *Financial statement analysis*. Wikipedia. Retrieved August 30, 2022, from https://en.wikipedia.org/wiki/Financial_statement_analysis#cite_note-WSF1997-1

higher than another. Anyone can see the variance between the budget and actual for an expense line or departmental result. It does not take a rocket scientist to see the discrepancy between this year's result and last year's. It also does not take an accountant to see the variance between the actual and forecast results and do something about it.

All the same, seeing the variance is one thing. Doing something about it is quite another. Most leaders will do nothing about it unless they are specifically told to do so. Most leaders will not naturally go there. Why is this the case?

Consider this:

Leaders typically see that variance as someone else's responsibility. Maybe accounting or some other magical entity will swoop in and make everything all right. Someone or something will come in and sprinkle some fairy dust on things and clean up the mess.

Leaders are too busy to bother with the numbers, and what is the point anyway? They are just numbers someone else created that really do not have anything much to do with leaders and their performance.

This kind of thinking is a problem—but it's masking the career opportunity you're looking for. Messes do not fix themselves. Messes will only ever be corrected if there is a joint effort. The problems reflected in the variances on the financials run deep. Is it the budget or forecast that is inaccurate? Is it the actual spend that is wrong because of timing or changes in the business needs? Are there items that are miscoded due to errors in the data or source documents? Is the alignment of the expenses correct to the budget and forecast plan?

So, where is the opportunity for the Operations Manager?

The opportunity is to become the leader that sees a problem, owns it, fixes it, and ultimately becomes a star because of it!

That is a big statement, but I want to tell you I have seen it happen many times. Most operations managers are new in their roles, and they are interested in one thing: Getting on their departmental horse and riding. That is one of the secrets in hospitality. We regularly "drain the swamp" and give a new leader a new shot at cleaning up the mess. The mess is always in need of cleaning up. That is the hotel business. Guest service and colleague engagement in that department you just took over needs your fresh set of eyes and heart. Well, guess what? The numbers need cleaning up, too, and the great news is that it is not a difficult task to get the numbers working for you.

If you just inherited a P&L section and it is a mess here is what to do:

Make friends with your payroll, accounts payable and purchasing people. Show them you are interested in helping get things right. They will love this because you just went from being on their list of managers to chase to the much shorter list of managers who have their act together. Now you have allies, and they are going to help you.

Stop the machine when it comes to the paperwork. Sit down with your invoices and POs and timesheets. Make sure that your processing lines up with the proper general ledger accounts (GL's). Your new friends in the administration will help you sort it all out. Just ask!

When it is your turn to submit the next month's forecast, take the time to have a deep look at what you are projecting. Chances are you do not have the zero-based detail to work from. This is where you put your stake in the ground. What is in the expense accounts and what is the staffing formula for your department? More on these concepts in future chapters.

So, clean up the swamp and what emerges from the former chaos is a new and vastly improved department, including the service, engagement and financial piece. You don't want to be the leader that misses this opportunity.

The second and more elusive opportunity comes from gaining perspective through financial statements. What is my business all about? How does what happens inside my business relate to what is on my financial statements? Here is a big clue for this piece, and it takes curiosity again. What are these numbers for? Why is certain information that you do not understand included in your departmental financials? Imagine looking at an interesting destination on a map and saying to yourself, "That place looks cool and interesting. I want to go there and check it out." Well, your financial statement is exactly the same. Everything included in your statement is there for a reason. It is part of the statement because it is material to the mission of effectively running your department. Get curious and find out what that information is and what it means—and then ask how can you learn from it.

I once worked with a young lady whom I will call Anne. She would come to me month after month with all the issues she found in her department's financials. It was really a mess—and so was the rest of her department. She never really complained about the content; rather than doing that she set about doing her piece to fix it, and like magic her understanding grew quickly. Before I knew it, she was telling me what it all meant—her version. Man, did it all get better fast in her department! Not long after that, she was promoted to manage another larger, more complicated, better-paying department. Today she is a GM. And she did not get there by accident. She got there through hard work, curiosity, and a willingness to drain the swamp.

These are the muscles you need to develop as a hospitality financial leader. It is not up to someone else (Accounting) to chase you down and to get you on top of your numbers. It is the other way around. The sooner you see the opportunity in all of this the better for you and your career. It is not difficult. If someone stands in your way, find a way around them. Like I said at the beginning of this chapter, most leaders will not naturally do this—will you be one who does?

If so, it will pave your road to greater personal career prosperity.

Chapter 25

Every Line Needs an Owner

My dear mother Donna often recited her favorite sayings, especially when she wanted to make a point. She had some really good sayings, and several have stuck with me. One of them I relate to hotel financial leadership. Her saying was, "Many hands make light work." How does that relate to creating an engaged leadership team in your hotel? Let me explain.

It is true in any aspect of our lives at home and work that teamwork makes things easier. The reason for this is that we have more effort directed toward the thing we are trying to do. The simplest example is trying to lift a heavy rock. If we work in a coordinated fashion and do it together, it is much easier.

In hotels, it is precisely the same with financial lifting. If the GM or Director of Finance tries to do it alone, it is hard—maybe even impossible.

But how do they get the others to lend a helping hand?

In hotels, you have an amazing tool to help you distribute the lifting. It is called the financial statement, or the P&L. What I want you to do with this tool is tear it apart and put it back together, giving every single line of revenue, cost of goods, payroll, expense and statistics to the appropriate manager or leader on your team. That's right, every single line. By using this strategy, you now have a blueprint of your business that shows who you need to communicate with when a certain line of a financial statement is out of whack.

Agreements need to be made with these individuals, so they clearly understand their role and responsibility regarding their lines of the statement. I assure you they have what they need to get the job done.

Once you have an owner for every line, you then need to work with these individuals to help them learn how to forecast and budget their lines each month. Once the forecast is consolidated, you now have a team member to call on if you need to make changes. You no longer tweak the forecast in a few areas to get the bottom line you need. You go back to the line owners and negotiate the changes.

So, stop right here.

I know what you are thinking: How is this possible or practical?

STOP!

This is the most important pivot in the creation of financial leadership. If you change the forecast for that line and give the consolidated forecast back to the team, and you have changed the line items without the agreement of the owner of that line, you have just fallen all the way back down the financial leadership ladder. You will have zero credibility with your leaders; they will quietly thumb their nose and flip their middle finger at you.

You are thinking you do not have time for this

Make the time and it will reward you handsomely.

The very essence of your hotel and financial leadership is built on this discipline. It is not possible to throw blankets at this and say, "Rooms will look after their accounts, and I will just deal with the Rooms Division Manager." Do not do this. It is not an effective strategy, because too many P&L lines intersect in your hotel—especially in rooms. Just sit down with the Rooms Division Manager and go through their statement with them and agree on who will be assigned each and every line.

Every line needs an owner!

A good example of the intersecting is a line like "guest supplies." Housekeeping, Front Desk, Concierge, Guest Service and even Sales spend money that ends up as an expense in this account. So who is the right individual to manage it? Do not be fooled into thinking the Rooms Division Manager will handle it. It will not happen. Get a name that you believe is the right person and make an agreement with the Rooms Division Manager regarding how this person is going to corral the others. This move is golden. The person you pick to quarterback this account must have great diplomacy and negotiation skills. You have just deputized a leader with a very important task, one that requires your commitment, patience, and resources.

Play this right and the leader will love you for this responsibility. Play it wrong and they will resist.

Make sure all other constituents who use mixed accounts know and agree that the owner of this account is the one who will prepare the zero-based budget and work equitably with all to make sure they know what they have to spend and when.

~

With most lines in the P&L, the owners are obvious. Take the time necessary to work with every single owner on their accounts. This is the foundation of your financial leadership in the hotel.

"Every line has an owner" will revolutionize your business—and the engagement of key players in your business. That is to say, if you invite the right people in, and in the right way, they will see their involvement as a vote of confidence and an opportunity to grow in their career.

This is your garden. Tend it and watch it grow.

III

MANAGING PAYROLL AND EXPENSES

In this section we get into the tools of the trade—that is, how to manage our costs, the payroll, and the expenses. If you're going to be successful in hospitality these two areas require mastery. No exceptions.

Chapter 26

Using EFTEs

If You Can't Measure It, You Can't Improve It.

Management thinker Peter Drucker is often quoted as saying, "You can't manage what you can't measure." Drucker means that you can't know whether or not you are successful unless success is defined and tracked.

In the hotel business, payroll is the number one cost. Smith Travel Research (STR) recently reported that labor costs equaled as much as 50% of revenues for a sample of over 4,000 hotels of all types and sizes. Having an efficient and reliable way to measure payroll is critical in any business. In hotels, the impact of payroll is significant, and the need to have a way to define and track it is key.

May I introduce the secret weapon and the star of the show? EFTEs!

Equivalent Full-time Employees.

I know from experience that most hotels do not include EFTEs in their daily reporting or on their financial statements. But it is a powerful metric. And you already have all the information you need to use it. You just need to organize it and let it tell you what's going on inside your hotel.

Measuring the dollars of payroll in your hotel is very important, but understanding productivity is by far the most powerful tool you have. Understanding and measuring productivity facilitates the comparison of like data. This is where the EFTE is so powerful. And it's not unique to the hotel world; many industries use this statistic.

Let's Define the Use of the EFTE

First, EFTEs measure the number of "equivalent" full-time employees. This is where most people get hung up. In the hotel business, we have full-time employees, part-time employees, salaried employees, hourly employees, unionized employees and even contracted labor. The EFTE calculation lets you see the **total** of these pieces of the hotel labor by area, department and overall. It also allows you to see the same information for a day, week, month or a year in a comparable way. This is very useful, and once you get started with EFTEs you are going to be hooked.

Let's Define the "Calculation" of the EFTE

This is the second most common place where people get hung up. If you can manage a little multiplication and division then this is very straightforward. Remember, the first word in the acronym is "equivalent."

To define one EFTE we need to start with the annual calculation. Once we understand the annual calculation we can reduce the same calculation for any month, week or single day in that year.

Now, do not go south on me with the following. Once you run this through your internal biocomputer you will get it. (I did, and as one good friend likes to remind me, I'm not always the sharpest knife in the drawer.)

For the basis of calculating an EFTE, we use 40 hours as the "equivalent" work week: 5 days x 8 hours per day. In hospitality, we all know most managers and leaders work more than 40 hours, so do not let this part confuse you.

The second part is the number of weeks in a year: $365/7 = 52.14$

For leap years we use: $366/7=52.29$

We then take our 40 hours and multiply it by our annual:

$$40 * 52.14 = 2086.$$

This is simply the number of hours a person working 5 days a week at 8 hours a day works in an entire year. Note here we do not factor in any holidays or vacation. We just want to know the number of hours one would work in an entire year.

From this magic number of 2086, we can figure out the daily and monthly EFTE values.

For a day, it's $2086/365 = 5.715$
For a month, it is the number of days in the month times 5.715
A month with 31 days is $31 * 5.715 = 177.1$
A month with 30 days is $30 * 5.715 = 171.5$
A month with 28 days is $28 * 5.715 = 160.0$

Now we know the basis for calculating the Equivalent Full-time Employee statistic for a given day, month and year.

Let's put it to work for your hotel.

There are two key areas in the hotel where you will want to see EFTEs in the reporting. These are:

1. Daily labor/productivity reports
2. Monthly financial statements

For the **daily reporting**, you only need to get the report from the time clock. Or, if there is a manual system, you need the "departmental hours worked" summary.

Then:

Take the daily hours worked by department and major classification and divide this number by the daily divisor of 5.715.
Next, divide the month-to-date hours by the month-to-date divisor.

Let's look at an example using housekeeping:

If daily hours worked in housekeeping are 185, then:

$$185/5.715 = 32.4 \text{ daily EFTEs.}$$

Month-to-date hours worked in housekeeping as of the 18th of the month:

$$3725 / (18*5.715) = 36.2 \text{ month-to-date EFTEs.}$$

This statistic can be used for any payroll calculation, big or small. From the number of EFTEs in the room attendant classification all the way to the total hotel EFTEs—it's all the same math. We will also want to apply this same view to the forecast, budget and previous year's values.

With the **monthly financial statements**, **annual budgets** and **monthly forecasts** we also want to incorporate EFTEs. You will need the right person to go under the hood and write the financial formulas for your reports. (This specialized person will be adept at coding financial systems and at getting data from one system to another; you will usually find them in your hotel's accounting department.) In addition, you will need to incorporate hours reporting on your monthly closing process. Create general ledger accounts to match each payroll classification you report on your financials. Run a monthly report from your time clock or post each pay period's hours, and do not forget to accrue the stub period and reverse the previous month's accrual. Once you get into the swing of booking the hours on your financials, it will be business-as-usual with EFTEs on your financial statements.

Imagine how much more insight you can gain from your business with EFTE reporting. With one glance, you can see the total EFTEs for the current year compared to the latest forecast for the next year. Look no further— now you can see the administration and general EFTE count, the food preparation EFTE count, the EFTE count for the actual, budget, forecast and previous year—all laid out side by side. Things are now much, much more clear in your financial reporting.

With hours reporting on daily reports and monthly financials, you can now introduce productivity reporting.

Watch a short video on "Calculating EFTEs"

https://qrco.de/bd6gcN

Chapter 27

Measuring Labor Productivity

It is important from the beginning to establish the goals for measuring productivity in your operations. This first section will focus on rooms, and the next will cover Food and Beverage (F&B).

Measuring productivity means we have two instruments we need to pay attention to at the same time. Like your sportscar's speedometer and tachometer. One tells you how fast the car is going; the other tells you how fast the car's engine is going—two very different but connected measures. With hotel labor productivity it's EFTEs and Hours Per Room or Hours Per Cover that we want to measure simultaneously.

Productivity in Rooms

The goal in measuring productivity in the rooms division is to see, monitor and ultimately improve on the number of hours of work it takes to service a room. The expression to use is **"hours per room occupied."**

"Hours worked divided by the number of rooms sold." This labor productivity statistic is the most important tool available to manage your biggest expense in the rooms division.

If you were making cars, you would want to know and continually improve on how many hours and minutes of labor it takes to make a car. Regarding rooms, labor comes down to how many hours it takes to service one room, which includes not just cleaning the room, but time related to reserving the room and other associated activities in the hotel, like checking in and out, concierge services, and so on. You want to see this at the total rooms level as well as how it breaks down.

The breakdown (or "stack") is best demonstrated with the following detailed subtotals of labor from each sub-department:

- Front office
- Housekeeping
- Room attendants
- Reservations
- Bell/door

These categories must be separate to see where there are productivity wins and challenges. To be able to see labor categories separately, use proper department and job codes so they fall into the different stacks. In addition to the separation of the stacks, you need to separate hourly and management positions in each stack.

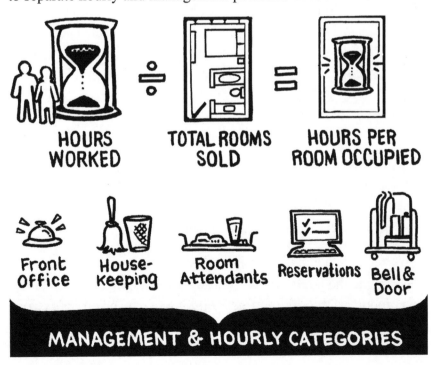

HOURS WORKED ÷ TOTAL ROOMS SOLD = HOURS PER ROOM OCCUPIED

Front Office   House-keeping   Room Attendants   Reservations   Bell & Door

MANAGEMENT & HOURLY CATEGORIES

To do this effectively and consistently, I recommend creating a kind of "payroll dictionary" that establishes a consistent way to segregate labor. Start by defining the difference between management and hourly positions in each sub-department. For consistency, ignore salaried versus hourly and union versus non-union. (These are ignored because they differ greatly from location to location.) Instead, focus on job title. The word "manager" is critical. If "manager" or higher appears in a category's title, this position falls into the **management category**. If "supervisor" or a lower title appears in the job title, the position falls into the **hourly category**. Here is an example for "front office." It is important to recognize that management or hourly terminology is only a way to organize data and is not an indication of any regard.

Front Office Stack

"Front Office Hourly"	**"Front Office Management"**
Front Office Clerks, Reception Clerks, Front Office Cashiers, Front Office Supervisor, Reception Supervisors, Night Audit Clerks, Secretary, Admin Assistant	Front Office Manager, Reception Manager, Assistant Manager, Front Office Director, Rooms Division Director, Night Manager and Assistant Night Mgr.

Repeat the same exercise and organize rooms department and positions into the different stacks and by the "hourly and management" classifications.

Once the classifications are established:

- track the hours worked in each stack
- divide the hours worked in each stack by the total number of rooms sold for the entire hotel: for one day, one month or one year.

Then you can capture the number of units of labor (hours of labor) it takes to sell the rooms and divide this by the number of units sold. You will have rock-solid data.

The **"hours per room occupied"** measurement can be used everywhere, starting with the annual budget. You will want to know the "hours per room occupied for the year" goal. For example, if the total hours for the rooms division in the budget is 45,978 and the total number of rooms occupied in the budget is 31,525 then the hours per rooms occupied is (45,978 / 31,525 = 1.4585). **This number, 1.4585, is gold!**

In everything you do with rooms labor, you now know the measure of success. Meet or beat the productivity goal of 1.4585 hours per room occupied and you win. If you can use this target in your daily schedule, weekly schedule and monthly forecast you can continually adjust course to track to your target.

Watch a short video on "Rooms Productivity"

https://qrco.de/bd6YdW

As the operations manager, you cannot have any impact on pricing or wages; they are out of your control. Any measurement that looks at labor as a percentage of sales is noteworthy, but you cannot control it. As the operations manager, what you have control over is the schedule and hitting the productivity target if sales volume is down or up. The "hours per room occupied" number is your speedometer, and you can tell what stacks are up to speed, which are not, and whether it is an hourly or management issue.

When you measure and track productivity this way you give leaders and managers on the ground a simple and effective tool. There will be days when you lose big on productivity goals. Days like Mondays in a leisure hotel. Challenging productivity days include days on which you have heavy arrival or departure, multiple occupancy, or low occupancy. On the other side of the coin, you will have days where productivity is naturally high: stay-overs, long-stay guests, business travelers, groups with heavy programs, and single occupancy guests.

What operations managers need to see is the hours-per-room-occupied goal. It's really the only productivity measure they need to focus on. Knowing there will be losses and wins in the days and weeks is natural. Hitting or beating the monthly productivity target is the magic result for operations managers to get excited about.

Productivity in Food and Beverage

In food and beverage, you want to get obsessed about a similar measurement of productivity, only we call it **"hours per customer cover served."**

Right out of the gate you need to understand the definition of a cover, and it has recently changed. A cover now properly refers to a "customer," and the "hours per customer cover served" is calculated by dividing the total sales in all food items by the total number of customers seated. We used to calculate only food sales divided by the number of people who actually ordered a food item. Now it's simpler in that the total of warm bodies in the restaurant is divided by total food sales.

So when it comes to measuring productivity, the number to get obsessed about is **"hours per customer."** Of course, unlike the cover in the rooms division, a "customer" can be more challenging to record consistently and correctly than a room sold. Be diligent with the food and beverage service staff to ensure they record their "customers" correctly in your point-of-sale system. Reviewing point-of-sale guest checks will tell you very quickly if this is being done properly and consistently. One other tip is to closely review the daily revenue report and look for average covers by meal period that do not make sense.

Productivity in F&B is also best measured by dividing **hours worked** by **customers served**. As already noted, operations managers have no control over wages or pricing, but they do have control over schedules, and this is where they should focus. The percentages and per cover/customer costs are important, but the trump card is hours per customer served. You need to see this measurement in all budgets, forecasts, daily reports, and schedules. What is the total productivity of F&B and how does it break down by outlet? You need stacks for each outlet that can stand on its own, and you also want to see the consolidated results.

In F&B there is a bigger challenge with productivity creation than in rooms. Because of the multiple departmental structures and the allocation of management, food preparation and stewarding, things must be set up a little differently. Again, you are going to need your payroll dictionary and different classifications based on job title.

The first delineation is the people in operations who work on the floor versus those who work behind the scenes. All service staff for an outlet, both management and hourly, are considered "direct." The hourly and management for food preparation, stewarding and F&B administration is considered "allocated." To design stacks in F&B, use the following structure.

Direct and Allocated Both Need Hourly and Management Positions:

Any Outlet Hourly Direct

All Wait Staff, Host, Bussers, Bartender, Bar Waiter, Cocktail Servers, Sommelier, Supervisors, Bar Backs, Captains, All Floor Guest Facing Non-Management Positions

Any Outlet Hourly Allocated

Cooks, Dishwashers, Kitchen Helpers, Apprentices, Supervisors, Pantry, Attendants, Porters, Cleaners, Chef de Partie, Butcher, Garde Manger, Secretary, Administrative Assistant, Office Clerk

Any Outlet Management Direct

Outlet Managers, Outlet Assistant Managers, Maître d', Beverage Manager, Assistant Manager

Any Outlet Management Allocated

Executive Chef, Sous Chef, Pastry Chef, Outlet Chef, Banquet Chef, All Chef Positions —Executive and Jr.

In banquets, there will be several additional hourly and management positions; however, the same hourly and management "allocated" positions will apply.

Banquets Hourly Direct

All Wait Staff, Porters, House Person, Bus Persons, Bar Person, Bartender, Banquet Supervisor, Banquet Captain, Banquet Bar Supervisor, Office Coordinator, Payroll Coordinator, Revenue

Clerk, Host, Hostess, Cashier, Banquet Secretary, Catering Coordinator, Administrative Assistant

Banquets Management Direct

Director of Banquets, Assistant Director of Banquets, Banquet Manager, Assistant Banquet Managers, Conference Services Managers, Assistant Conference Services Managers, Catering Managers, Assistant Catering Managers

The value created by these groupings and classifications is well worth the effort.

In food and beverage, **you cannot get away from the allocation game.** In your hotel, the most efficient way to manage your food and food labor costs is to have one main kitchen that prepares cold food, sauces, soups, pastries, banquets, butchers the meat, etc., and then an outlet kitchen that prepares the final product—usually the protein—through a combination of resources from the main kitchen's efforts and their own.

The same idea is applied to stewarding and administration in the F&B division. Hotels that try to capture all the costs for food and labor directly for each outlet are ultimately not successful. They either spend too much time creating the separation and end up duplicating efforts, or they pretend that they can capture the actual costs.

Either way, allocations of labor and cost of goods are inevitable.

In the end, the allocation method is ultimately the most efficient way to manage labor in food and beverage.

In food and beverage, what you need is an effective way to measure and manage. The **"direct and allocated/management and hourly"** is the way to go.

Have a daily labor analysis produced so you can track and monitor productivity. Include these summaries in the financial statements each month. From that analysis, you can see where the hotel is winning with productivity and where it is not.

Watch a short video on "F&B Labor Productivity"

https://qrco.de/bd6XFS

Chapter 28

Top 10 Labor Controls

To say labor cost is important is an understatement. Managing labor costs is a never-ending battle in any hotel. In this chapter I will highlight some key controls and features to help you make sure you are on the right track with this all-important aspect of hospitality. You can use the list below to come up with new action plans to tackle labor costs in your operation

10. Updated Daily Occupancy Forecast

If the people in the departments inside your hotel do not have an up-to-date and accurate forecast for rooms occupied, arrivals and departures, you are missing an important feature. Even if the report they have is a day old, you are behind and flying with one eye shut. Always make sure your team leaders have and use the latest forecast and, where possible, adjust the schedules daily.

9. Labor Reporting Daily and MTD

As quoted above, the famous economist Peter Drucker coined the phrase, "You can't manage what you can't measure." Pretty simple and straightforward thinking: we must measure the results if we want to get better. On top of that thought, I offer the following—Monson's Law: "When performance is measured, performance improves. When performance is measured and reported back, the rate of improvement accelerates." – Thomas S. Monson. So, there you have it. We must include daily and month-to-date reporting in our efforts to manage labor cost.

8.   Quarterly Review of All Schedules

There are no new tricks, just people who practice them. An old boss of mine taught me this one. Every quarter we would have a special meeting where each manager had to present their department's schedules to him and the rest of the leadership team. We never left that room without serious savings. The way he looked at it was simple: labor creep is everywhere, and the best way to stop it is "peer review."

7.   Include It in Your Financials

Include the labor cost and fully report the payroll numbers as well as the statistics in your monthly financial statements, budgets and forecasts.

6.   Budget and Forecast It

To really bring the entire payroll piece into play in your hotel, plan your entire financial picture using all the available tools in your annual budgets and monthly forecast in detail. If you leave it out, or even just a part of it, you are not fully embracing the spirit or the importance of fully and effectively managing this beast. Don't only go halfway. Fully report wages, supplemental and benefits, and also be sure to include the stats for EFTEs and productivity. Once you have it all together you will wonder how you ever existed without it.

5.   Use EFTEs

The clue was in number 6. Using EFTEs in all of your labor reporting, including daily, month-to-date as well as budgets and forecasts, will transform your management culture. I also know what you are thinking if you don't currently use these tools, that they are complicated and too much. Well, that is simply not true. If you can multiply and divide you have what you need to run with EFTEs. [4]

4. Knowing What You Can Control

Managing labor effectively means we need to understand what we can control and what we cannot. Time and time again I hear people talking about labor cost as a percentage of revenue. Please stop this useless practice. You don't control how much most of your employees are paid—the local government or the union does. You also don't control how many customers come through the door or what they pay, because average rates go up and down. But you do control the schedule, so focus on scheduling effectively using productivity measures, not labor dollars divided by revenue.

3. Embrace Hours Per Room Occupied and Per Customer Cover Served

These two battle cries must be the leading move in any attempt to manage and report labor in your hotel. These stats are constants that do not get impacted by wage movements or increases or decreases in pricing. Cut straight to the chase and measure productivity and stop confusing people with labor cost percentage, which should only be used as after-the-fact, anecdotal information.

2. Schedule Using Hours Per Room Occupied or Cover Served

The real pros know that managing labor means getting and staying on top from the get-go. That translates into scheduling using the

---

[4] Pro tip: Get a copy of my EFTE and productivity exercise by sending me an email requesting it, and then teach your team!

productivity measures in number 3. Knowing your productivity targets by labor area and scheduling effectively is the only way to fly. Knowing that your goal is to meet or beat the productivity target at month-end or year-end is the game. Playing and winning the game with productivity measures is like baseball—you don't need to win every inning; it is the accumulated results at the end that count.

1.   Staffing Guides

Make sure every department has a freshly prepared one—at least an annual staffing guide that includes an approved list of fixed/salaried positions as well as a formula for every hourly position. Also, make sure it is used and is accurate. Test it often. Don't overlook or take for granted this all-important document. Make sure all of your managers are fluent with their staffing guides and that they use them.

The hotel business and being effective with labor productivity is a game of inches that add up to major dollars at the end of the month and year. Take each issue to task and realize this is a never-ending exercise that you can use to your advantage.

Watch a short video on the "Top 10 Productivity Killers in Your Hotel"

https://qrco.de/bd6e4A

Chapter 29

Zero-Based Expenses: How to Plan and Manage

In the hospitality world, there are only two main cost types that need a system and strategy to properly control them: payroll and expenses. In this chapter I am going to talk about expenses—namely about creating a process for establishing and managing your expenses on an ongoing basis, in real-time, using a zero base. Although this chapter might seem like it is largely directed at hotel General Managers and Directors of Finance, managers of individual departments can use the same formula as everyone else in a hotel, and this helps create a smoother system.

A zero-based budget requires justifying every line item. When creating one, you start from scratch—from zero—and work your way up from there. This is typically done once every year.

You might think that in large hotels the zero base would be very hard to establish but, in my experience, it's just the opposite. It's actually easy to find and define the details. One problem is that the task itself competes with the other business tasks—such as guest requirements. The challenge becomes pulling it all together when everyone's busy with the task of running the hotel. But if this work takes a backseat to operations, hotels can end up operating without a concrete plan for managing their expenses.

Oddly enough this situation might be okay for most hotel managers, but owners have a very different view. General managers are interested in keeping things fluid and smooth. This means they can operate with a certain amount of flexibility, and their spending reflects this. After all, the total revenues are coming in, and we all know that a certain amount of volume and revenue can hide a multitude of sins—as long as plenty of money is coming in, no one is too concerned about the exact details of the money—even though they should be! At least that's the case until the customers slow down or, heaven forbid, the phone stops ringing. When it does, or when the hotel chooses to make the effort to control their expenses, the system they need to use is the tried and true zero base.

In order to establish a zero base, we need to do some homework— nothing too complicated, but it requires focus and some discipline. All too often the task of getting the details is left to a junior "somebody." This is a mistake. Teaching your "juniors" the system once it's established is a good idea, but getting this process working correctly requires an individual who can organize and allocate resources within their department—this means you need someone seasoned.

To establish the zero base, we need to create our list for each general ledger account in complete detail. The best way to do this is to run the line-by-line from each account for the prior twelve months. Once we know the vendors, we then pull the corresponding invoices and record the items purchased as well as the quantities and unit prices.

This is not rocket science, and it may sound tedious, but there is no other way.

Once this is done you have your detail, and now it's time to plan. What are the parameters of your expense budget and the historical cost for this expense line? From your research and your knowledge of how your department operates what do you need to include in your forecast? For example, if the account title is "guest amenities" it might include shampoo, mouthwash, toothbrushes and so on. This information may change from year to year; for example, individual shampoo bottles might be replaced by shampoo dispensers. Make your plan and include all the items, prices, and quantities. Take into account the forecasted occupancy or the cover counts for rooms or F&B. For non-operating departments, it's total revenue you want to measure your expenses against.

From the forecast of each line, we now have the departmental total expense forecast for the month in front of us. We submit the totals for each line to the finance leaders and they consolidate our data with all the other departments. When this is done it's inevitably too many dollars of expense; this is the pivot point, and the most important part of the exercise so far.

You may be asked to reduce your department's expenses by a dollar value. Let's say a $5,000 reduction is requested. Now you have a list to look at and you get to decide what you can live without next month. Remove these items from your forecast detail and retain a record of what was axed.

Now you have the detail to support the forecasted dollars of expenses, and it's time to start ordering your supplies. This is another critical juncture, because we want to ensure our spending is in keeping with the revenue projections. In most hotels, we book a significant portion of our revenues in the room's area "in the month, for the month." We need to order in one- or two-week installments, allowing for the ability to reduce or even increase quantities needed based on the pick-up. This is why we do the zero-based work: it gives us the ability to flex our spending based on revenues, allowing our department to manage its flow thru.

If the forecast was for 75% occupancy and a rate of $150, and the projection on the fifteenth of the month is 70% and $145, I need to adjust my ordering and expenses to compensate for the drop in revenues. If I don't have my detailed list, I'm sunk, and I have no way of knowing what to trim.

I have a section in my workshops where we discuss zero-based expense planning, and I explain it like a household grocery shopping experiment. It goes like this: if I send you to the store with $200 and ask you to buy some groceries, you will spend the $200 and come home with lots of interesting things. On the other hand, if I send you to the store with the same cash and a shopping list you will come home with what's on the list.

Now the pivot. I only have $180 this week, so I send you to the store with the same list and I ask you to decide what we can live without this week. Now we have a chance to get what we really need for groceries, given our revised forecast. Your hotel departmental expenses control and your zero-based system are the same.

It's just being organized and having a list. With that list, you're going to know what you need, what to order and, if need be, what to trim. It's not rocket science. In fact, the biggest mystery is why this isn't standard practice at more hotels.

Don't let yours be one of them—get on board with zero-based expenses budgeting.

Watch this short video on using "Zero-Based Expenses"

https://qrco.de/bd6YQN

Chapter 30

Using Expense Checkbooks

I can vividly remember being a young lad and watching my dad sitting at the kitchen table paying the monthly bills by check, and then updating his checkbook. I remember asking him why he entered the details on the page at the back of the checkbook. He said very clearly, "So we don't spend more than we have in the bank. If I don't keep track, we'll run out of money and I'll end up bouncing a check!"

In hospitality, and as department heads (or GMs setting standards for department heads) we are all much better off when we use the checkbook system to manage our expenses so we don't overspend. The only difference between my dad's and your department's expenses is that you don't really run out of money—you just go over your budget or forecast. This usually results in some frustration, perhaps even a nasty email or two. The great thing about this situation is that it can easily be rectified with a little work on your part. Having and using a checkbook is a great way to stay on top of your departmental expenses. Do this and your star shines.

Contrary to common belief, a useful and accurate checkbook does not require a computer system and, in many cases, it is much easier to use one without all the hoopla that an online environment creates. All you need is a piece of paper. And of course, if you want to use a computer, a simple Excel spreadsheet will do nicely.

The basic idea about a checkbook is to tell the user what the final position is with your line-by-line expenses and exactly where you are on that path. Specifically:

- What has been ordered (including approved and ordered purchases)?
- What has been received (goods received that have invoices or packing slips that were signed and sent to accounts payable)?
- What has been received but which does not have an invoice or packing slip (items that need to be accrued at month-end, items that need to be added to the expenses)?

The checkbook must be organized so you have a different list (page) for each general ledger account you are responsible for—for example, guest supplies, cleaning supplies, paper goods, and so on.

The first thing to do is make a separate page for each account and put a title on it. Next, populate each sheet with the items you will need to order. Here is where most people tune out—but not you. If you are not sure what to write for the items you need to order, do the following: write down the items you think you need. After the month starts and you order additional items, write those down on the correct page. If you do this, your list by account will come together very quickly. When you make an order, be sure to write the dollar amount in the "ordered" column. Tip: Add the quantity to the item's column with the description. This will be a great help next month.

Once the order has been placed, the next step is to simply wait for the items to arrive. When they do, enter the dollar amount in the "arrived" column. Normally, items arrive with an invoice or packing slip. Make sure you see this and sign it, and I also recommend you make a scan or photocopy for your records. The signed slip will either go to the receiving department or it will be your job to get it to the accounts payable person. When this happens you write the amount of the goods received in the "invoice signed" column. If you do this for all the items and services you order, you will have a full checkbook of the items ordered, received and approved for payment.

DATE	EXPENSE	ORDERED	RECEIVED w/INVOICE	RECEIVED NO INVOICE	ACCRUAL
MAR 15	Laundry Detergent	$250.⁰⁰	$250.⁰⁰	–	$0
MAR 17	Printer Paper	$130.⁰⁰		$130.⁰⁰	$130
MAR 18	Toliet Paper	$150.⁰⁰			$0

The last step is to accrue any items received that did not have an invoice or a packing slip. All you are doing with the accrual is telling the accounting department that these goods or services were received in the current month and no invoice was received. Using this information, the accounting department will bring these expenses into the current accounting period.

Now that you have one month under your belt, you're off to the races. You now have a base for all your expense lines. You now know where things go—into which account—and how much you spent. From this point forward, each month you add to your knowledge and accuracy. Do not worry about missing items, especially in the beginning. Just start—and pull your list together.

This is the hardest part—the beginning. Remember the golden rule about budgeting and forecasting: the only thing we know for sure is that the number we come up with is wrong. That's right—your forecast will never be perfect. It is always going to be a work in progress, but knowing what you ordered, what has come in and what you have signed off on is career gold. You will very quickly organize your departmental expenses and make a name for yourself with the people who can tell everyone in your hotel that you have your "$%#@" together.

This is what you want. Not the chaos that comes from not knowing in detail what your expenses are. Do not be the one who misses this opportunity to shine.

Be the leader who has and uses their hospitality financial leadership skills.

IV

COST OF GOODS AND FOOD AND BEVERAGE CONTROLS

"Food and beverage" (F&B) is different. Not all hotels have F&B offerings, but full-service hotels in some instances have many offerings. F&B is special because it's a big and complicated landscape that requires discipline to tame. Everyone likes to eat, and most enjoy a drink, so wrapping your arms around your understanding in this area is critical to your success in hospitality.

Chapter 31

Global Food Cost versus Tracking Individual Outlet—Pros and Cons

F ood cost calculations answer the question: what did the food cost us for the revenue we're able to make from it? There are two ways to do food cost calculations in your hotel. The first involves calculating the global cost of goods sold (COGS). The second involves tracking food costs for individual outlets (the hotel restaurant, the coffee shop in the lobby, room service, etc.). The first method works best, and ought to be standard operating procedure for hotels.

The second is a waste of time!

Despite this, I often find people trying to track individual outlet costs based on requisitions. Now, requisitions serve a valuable function at times, but not in terms of calculating costs.

The "global food costs" figure refers to the total food cost for the hotel, including the food costs for the individual outlets. It takes into account all the food that's delivered to the hotel and kept in the main kitchen or the storeroom. People tend to think that the costs come when the food is requisitioned and sent to an outlet, but of course the real cost is the inventory that's arrived at the hotel.

Ultimately, food cost is calculated by adding the opening inventory to the purchases, and then subtracting the closing inventory and any legitimate credits at month end. Doing this by outlet is completely inefficient, and we'll see why below.

What I see time and time again is people trying to track individual outlet costs using the direct issues and purchases to the outlets. However, there is always a catch at the end of the month: we have to use the cost of sales adjustment to book the correct inventory value, and when we do, we have an additional cost that must be charged to an outlet. Invariably we end up back where we started with a global food cost.

When I do my monthly financial statements, part of my task involves counting the remaining inventory. Then I need to do a cost of sales adjustment to get the inventory value. This formula is:

opening inventory + purchases – closing inventory

The reality is that the food cost is determined by the cost of sales/global food costs, and not by requisitions.

When the end of the month rolls around, what matters in terms of calculations is what's left in inventory in the storeroom/main kitchen. This is because that's where all the food originates and where much of the basic food is prepared. Items like pastries, salads, and sauces are just some examples of food that is almost always prepared in the central kitchen and then distributed to the outlets. On top of that, the same kitchen typically provides room service. Quite often, too, for all practical purposes the all-day outlet and bar are serviced by the main kitchen. There is also an extension for the banqueting kitchen from the main kitchen, and often they are one and the same.

So there is no reason to calculate food costs related to outlet sales, because it's duplication of effort. Food costs come out in the global calculation. The requisitions to the main kitchen and storeroom are important in terms of figuring out what items are popular and that sort of thing, but they will not help you calculate global food costs. In fact, if you rely on the requisitions to calculate costs you will only get an incomplete picture. Oftentimes food is requisitioned but not used. For example, if too much food is prepared and not enough ordered, or if the cream for the coffee stand goes bad, or if the barista gives the charming customer a free pastry . . . we'll end up with requisitioned food that doesn't bring in cash. In these instances, the requisitions are valuable for data other than costs, but they will only confuse the global food costs calculation.

Think of it this way. If you're trying to calculate the monthly food costs for your home kitchen, you will keep a tally of what you spend at the grocery store every month. You bring your groceries home and put them in your refrigerator and cupboards. It doesn't make any difference whether you eat the food at home, send it with your kids to school or take it on a picnic. Even if it spoils and has to be thrown away, your global food cost is still based on what you brought home from the grocery store.

So why do some hotels waste their time and effort requisitioning and tracking the food in a perpetual way only to have to fall back to the global cost calculation at the end of the month?

I am convinced that some of the people who make the rules do not understand how the accounting process must always end with the cost of goods calculation. We're just spinning our wheels with wasted effort if we're tracking individual outlet costs each month.

But I want to make sure people understand the reality of the situation. Especially given the fact that hotels are forever looking for ways to be more efficient. I have seen hotels that have several full-time employees dedicated to the task of tracking the food costs, even though it's all for naught. In my own time "on the inside" I worked in two very large hotel F&B operations. One had a system where we actually attempted to do individual outlet food costs.

What a waste of time! Especially when it dawned on me what was really going on. We were four people in the F&B control office, and each month we diligently tracked and posted all the requisitions from the storerooms to the outlets. At the end of the month, we would send the accounting department the figures.

I actually thought that that would be the end of the story, but it never was.

Each month the accountant tossed our requisition figures in the trash. He would only look at the closing inventory once all the purchases were booked. It was not until a few years later when I was taking some accounting classes that I figured out what he was doing and why.

What hotels should do—to conserve effort and create an accurate picture of costs—is create a requisition process whereby food is requested from the main kitchen by the outlets, and then the food is issued by the main kitchen or by the storeroom. This way the operations people can see the costs of the food "in circulation." A careful analysis of these requisitions from time to time will provide an indication of the direct costs involved, and this is useful information because it tells them what they're ordering—how much, frequency, etc.—but it is never complete or 100% of the food the outlet consumes. And it's not necessary for calculating global food costs; it's not the same thing. It's useful information, but it does not provide a complete picture.

If you are working in a hotel that is trying to track individual outlet food costs—good for you. But I am willing to bet you the cost of a visit to your hotel that it is not the end of the food cost story or calculation in your hotel. You may want to take this up with the individual who produces your financial statement for an eye-opening experience, and you might also want to ask yourself if all the work being done to track the food is really worth the effort.

Chapter 32

Food and Beverage Costs or Contribution Margin?

The concepts in this chapter apply to both food and beverages; however, I'm using beverages as my example.

We hear about it every month: the beverage cost! Usually, it's not pretty. It's always too high, and it typically creates lots of finger-pointing and pontificating. Beverage cost calculations are always a slightly complex beast, and the process of getting the right figures is often misunderstood. This is largely because this poor cousin to food cost is shrouded in a bit of mystery and mystique, like a secret cocktail recipe.

But a major key to profitability in F&B is *learning to offer first what profits the most.* So, the really important concept to understand when it comes to beverage sales is "contribution margin." This helps you determine which drinks bring in the biggest dollar profit. In this chapter I'll show you how to calculate the contribution margin of individual beverages, and then you can share this information with the people who need to know it.

Booze is the primary driver here, and we have three main categories of it to consider:

- Liquor
- Beer
- Wine

A possible fourth category is "minerals"—which includes soft drinks, tonic water and so on. These are often used in creating cocktails, for example. But mineral sales are generally much smaller, and their contribution margin is consequently less relevant, so to keep this discussion more manageable we can safely set them aside for the moment.

Like most people's children, these three categories of drinks all look and behave very differently. And what's important to consider in this discussion is not so much cost as *contribution*.

Contribution is measured two ways. The first is the inverse of the cost divided by the selling price minus one. So, if your cost for a drink is $2.50 and you sell it for $10.00, the formula will look like this:

$2.50 (cost) / $10 (selling price) = 1-25% = 75% (profit/contribution margin)

If this seems confusing, read on for more comparisons and it will become more clear. I teach this material in my workshops, and I occasionally get the same feedback in the beginning. There can be a bit of a learning curve, but stick with it.

Contribution Margin of Liquor

Let's look at some specific drinks. We'll start with a vodka tonic—a well-known member of the liquor family.

Let's say we pour 1.5-ounce drinks in my establishment. A 26-ounce bottle of Smirnoff costs our hotel $8. We get 17.3 pours out of one bottle when we sell highballs (26 / 1.5 = 17.3).

We sell each highball for $8. My portion cost is $8 divided by 17.3, the number of pours:

$$$8.00 / 17.3 = 46.2 \text{ cents}$$

My contribution margin in this example is **94.2%**.

Another way to establish the contribution margin is to express this as:

$$\$8.00 - .462 = \$7.53$$

In my liquor highball example, we produce a gross contribution of \$7.53 and a gross contribution margin of 94.2%, or, inversely, a cost of 5.8%.

Contribution Margin of Beer

Now for the second example: contribution margin of beer.

If a bottle of beer costs me \$2.05 and I sell it for \$6.00, the math is. $(2.05 / 6.00) = 34.2\% - 1 = 65.8\%$. My contribution margin on this example is 65.8%, my beer cost is 34.2%.

Another way to establish the contribution margin is to express this as $(6.00 - 2.05 = 3.95)$.

In the beer example, we produce a gross profit of \$3.95 and a gross contribution margin of **65.8%**.

Contribution Margin of Wine

The third and final part of the family we will look at is the **contribution from wine**. In this example, we will use house wine.

My house white wine costs \$12 per one-liter bottle and I sell a glass for \$11. I pour a 5-ounce portion. There are 35 ounces in a one-liter bottle, so I get 7 glasses per bottle. (When I serve wine, I want to use a 5-ounce carafe or a portioning device to ensure my quantities are always correct.)

My cost is $(\$12 / 7 = \$1.71)$. My contribution margin on this example is 84.5%. My beverage cost is 15.5%.

Another way to establish the contribution markup is to express this as $(11.00 - 1.71 = \$9.29)$. In the house wine example, we produce a gross profit of \$9.29 and a gross contribution margin of **84.5%.**

Portion Control

You can see from the above that accurate portion control is

essential. In another chapter we'll discuss this in greater depth, but it's clear that having methods in place to accurately track portions is key to profitability.

Summary

To summarize: we have liquor, beer and wine all behaving very differently:

Liquor cost of $.42 per portion, beverage cost of 5.8%, gross profit of **$7.53, and a contribution margin of 94.2%**
Beer cost of $2.05 per portion, beverage cost of 34.2%, gross profit of **$3.95, and contribution margin of 65.8%**
Wine cost of $1.71 per portion, beverage cost of 15.5%, gross profit of **$9.29, and contribution margin of 84.5%**

It should be clear from this why knowing a drink's contribution margin is highly relevant to understanding profitability. You can see, for example, that although your dollar profit from wine is higher than that from liquor, liquor's cost percentage is actually better. This is what most people get hung up on—fixating on a lower percentage. We have to remember we take dollars to the bank, not percents. It is interesting to consider, too, that profitability doesn't equate to charging the customer as much as possible; you can see this again with the highball example, in which even though they are paying less for their highball than a glass of wine, the drink is still highly profitable for the hotel.

Getting the Information into the Right Hands

Who in your establishment should know and understand this? Who knows which products produce the highest margins and which ones to sell first? Primarily the servers in the restaurants and the catering managers; the former because they take the orders from customers, the latter because they sell the group events. Think about your local car dealer. They know which car models have the biggest markups and the highest contribution margins. Your beverage operation is no different. This intel should be front and center.

In your restaurants and bars, do your servers know what products to offer first? Do they understand the difference between the contribution margin and the beverage cost? I bet most of them do not. You now have an excellent tool to use to help get your service staff to sell the most profitable items first.

Make sure colleagues like your food and beverage manager are well aware of these details. Convey the information to your restaurant and bar managers. You may need to sit down with various individuals to teach these and other principles, particularly if you notice something wrong in areas of profitability and cost versus contribution margins. The most important part is to train people to understand and, when it makes sense, to sell the most profitable thing first.

In your banquet and catering operation, what products are your sellers actively promoting? Clients often know exactly what they want, but there are also many instances in which they are looking for suggestions, help, and service. So, when a client presents with a budget figure and needs your help putting together their event, you have an excellent opportunity to steer them in the highest profit direction. (I am not suggesting you deceive or take advantage of them—as noted above, the highest profit for the hotel is not always related to how much a customer is charged.)

Learn to offer first what profits the most. When it comes to beverage cost, the contribution margin is the key factor, and understanding it leads to greater profits.

Watch a short video on "Understanding Contribution Margin"

https://qrco.de/bd6YtP

Chapter 33

Separating Group and Local Sales in Banquets

If your hotel has a reasonable amount of meeting space (+10,000 ft) and your banquet business is a significant contributor in your Food and Beverage Department (+20% of F&B revenue), you are going to want to separate local banquet business from group banquet business on all of your financial statements, forecasts, budgets and daily reporting.

"Why would I want to do that?" you might be asking. "That sounds like a lot of work." There are some very good reasons to make this standard practice in your hotel. I see many hotel financial statements, and most are missing the boat in this area. Separating this reporting and setting it up properly provides powerful information you can use in your hotel to make better decisions and ultimately be more profitable. When you take the process apart and look at each piece, it is not complicated. It just requires someone who wants to do it. Let's look at why it makes sense to set up separate revenue reporting for groups and locals inside your banquet department."

The first reason is to track the revenue and follow the profitability.

You want to know how much banquet revenue is generated by groups in-house who occupy your bedrooms versus the revenues generated by local customers who use your hotel's meeting rooms and banquet facilities, but don't occupy guest rooms.

We normally refer to the business coming from in-house groups as *Conference Service*. We call the business that comes from customers who do not occupy rooms as *Catering*, and we also call them *Group* and *Local*.

If a significant portion of your F&B revenue comes from banquets, there is a very good chance that you have two competing elements inside this revenue stream. You want to know how much revenue comes from each separate element. In rare circumstances (like a remote resort without significant local business) this separation may not be necessary. All other hotels that have a good mix of business would benefit from reporting this data separately.

You want to know the revenue separation for all types of sales in the banquet department. The following areas need separate reporting: food, beverage, room rental, audio visual, gratuities and miscellaneous.

Groups Versus Local

You need to understand the spending characteristics of these two different customers so you can choose your customers wisely. If you are running a full-service banquet and meeting facility and, on top of it, you have a few hundred bedrooms to sell, you want to use the meeting and banquet facilities to drive room nights. When you do not have opportunities to fill your hotel with groups, you want to be able to sell your space to local customers who want to hold meetings and events without staying at your hotel.

Understanding the spending and profit potential that each different element produces will help you develop your strategy for selling to groups versus local business. What does the average customer spend in local catering versus in-house groups? What are your minimum food and beverage sales per room occupied for your in-house groups? What is the minimum amount spent on food and beverage to release the main ballroom or other anchor rooms in your hotel? An essential element to properly manage your hotel is understanding these characteristics and the corresponding seasonality. Separating the revenues is the only way to go.

When you review your financials, budgets and forecasts you need to understand the makeup of the entire revenue picture in your hotel. Groups versus transient and corporate room revenue and local versus in-house banquet business creates a different picture each month, week and day in your hotel.

Understanding what it will take to drive the maximum revenues and profits starts with understanding the piece of business that is going to bring you the greatest contribution of both and at what time of year. In most hotels with significant meeting space, it is group business; when these group opportunities are minimal, like summer, holidays and weekends, you want to sell your space to local catering customers. Therefore, you need to separate financial revenue reporting within the banquet department to measure your effectiveness. If you lump it all together, as many hotels do, you are missing a huge opportunity to better understand and manage your business.

The second reason you want to separate these numbers is to organize your team—sales, conference services and catering—so you can sell and service the business most effectively.

This is where the water quite often gets murky.

Depending on how you organize your efforts in catering and conference services, you probably have people dedicated to one or the other—or, in some cases, both group and local elements. In your sales department for rooms, you have sales managers with segments to sell into, quotas to meet, and bonuses to earn. These sales quotas must contain food and beverage spending minimums. This is a critical policy that many hotels waver on with groups in certain "need periods"—such as a very slow month in which occupancy is low.

In conference services, you want to know how much revenue each seller and each group is generating. You want to have intel so you can see the overall spending of each in-house group. You want to know how much revenue is produced by each catering manager. These leading indicators help you maximize your revenues and profits. If you do not know how much revenue each seller in the various areas is producing, how will you know how effective they are and what more is possible in this area?

Are you leaving money on the table by not having enough sellers in each area? Are the efforts of each seller today producing enough revenue to justify their positions? Are your F&B spending parameters effective and do they adjust seasonally to reflect your change-in-business mix? Do your catering minimums and room rental policies reflect the most up-to-date data? Most hotels cannot tell you these important statistics. The main reason is that they do not separate group and local business reporting.

On top of all this is the six-thousand-pound rhinoceros in any hotel that has significant group business mixed with local banquet demand. How and who controls the meeting space in your hotel? What tools do they have to help them decide when to release banquet space for local business and when to hold onto it to sell to groups?

Are you organized to make the best decisions for the hotel?

In most hotels, this is a hotly contested subject. Most hotels have some guidelines but when you dig into the policy for meeting space versus room nights versus room revenue versus banquet revenues versus group spending versus local spending versus the profitability for each element, you are not going to find much in the way of evidence to win your case. You will find a lot of opinions but not a lot of facts to back them up.

Having these spending and room night guidelines by season, by day of the week, and by segment, with an effective review process, is the picture you want to build. By building this structure in your banquet department you will start to develop your revenue management muscles. The combined rooms and banquets, groups and local revenue management intelligence in your hotel is the result.

Creating the system to separate these two revenue streams in your banquet department is not difficult. It begins with how you organize your selling and servicing of groups, their corresponding banquet event orders (BEOs) and separate codes for group versus local. Next, it is a point-of-sale (POS) system that has separate revenue buckets for the group and local sales. These are easily set up. You need floor staff who are trained to post the banquet sales to the corresponding codes from the BEOs. You also need to review the final invoice versus the BEOs to ensure that all revenues are posted correctly.

Next, you need to set up daily reporting for the group and local sales on your daily flash reports. Your monthly financial statements and general ledger need to be programmed to have separate codes and reporting for the group and local sales inside the banquet department. Monthly forecasts and annual budgets that include analysis and reporting are also necessary.

Summing It all Up

Track and report your banquet group and local business separately. Do this on all your financial reports, daily, monthly and annually. Budget and forecast these revenue streams separately. Track and manage these revenue streams by the seller. These disciplines will lead you to full-blown revenue management processes that integrate rooms with banquets.

Understand your business better with the right data and you will make better selling decisions and increase your overall hotel profitability.

Watch a short video on "Separating Group and Local Sales in your Banquet Department"

https://qrco.de/bd6Yxx

Chapter 34

The 80/20 Rule and Food Cost

We have all heard of the 80/20 rule. But I am willing to bet most of you have not heard it in conjunction with the words "food cost."

A good friend of mine who was an Executive Chef explained it to me, and I am going to share it with you.

The 80/20 rule states that 80% of any result comes from 20% of the activity. In food cost, what my friend taught me is that 80% of the food cost comes from only 20 items. That's right—the top 20! Identify the top 20 food items your hotel buys using the dollar value of those items. It takes a bit of work, but once you have your list it is impressive. In the hotel we worked in, the gross food purchases were over $10 million. The test identified our top 20: bacon, sausage, cream, butter, OJ, dinner rolls, beef tenderloin, shrimp 16-20 count, individual yogurt, tomatoes, eggs, ground beef, halibut, chicken breasts, french fries, smoked salmon, coffee, lettuce, rib eye and brie cheese. Sure enough the 80/20 rule was right. We had over $7 million worth of these items purchased in one year.

My friend's way of managing the costs of these items is magic. Each month, on a rotating basis, everyone focuses on one of the top 20 items. The sous chefs, purchasing department, stores, catering, conference services and outlet managers all focus on that one item. When the entire team focuses on one food item and how to improve on buying it, storing it, cooking it and serving it, positive things almost always happen.

So, every twenty months, he turns over the list. This keeps everyone on their toes, including the suppliers. When they get in on the game, they come up with new and innovative products. Everyone knows the food item of the month, and it is like a mini-competition to find savings. He sends suppliers a note each month with the annual quantity of the "monthly focus item" they purchase and a request to have the suppliers look for a better product. Suppliers love to help and really respond, especially when they know other suppliers are receiving the same request.

Some months ago he told me that with the changes he made one month, the hotel would save $100K next year. Once you see the volume of your top 20 and find ways to innovate, your savings are multiplied.

Some of the ideas come from the strangest places. Catering suggested the tenderloin be tested. The director of catering bought AA at home and did not think the AAA was worth the difference. Would a grade less be just as good? They brought in samples and did a blind tasting and—voila!—60,000 lbs. of tenderloin just went from $24.99 a pound to $21.99. You do the math.

Another month it was orange juice. The idea was: Why can't we get it in a bigger portion than the 2-liter containers? Sure enough the supplier came back with a 4-liter container. The switch equated to savings of over $30K.

Be careful not to make this just an exercise in math. A lower price is good but the quality and consistency need to be there. Let the chef decide, and also allow a higher-priced product if they feel it's superior and desirable.

Your Vendors Need to Work for You

Continually ask your vendors to seek out new and better items from their suppliers. That is their job: to keep you happy and buying. Know your top 20 and pull your team together to innovate. Find out what your competitors are using. Pick up the phone and call three of your competitors. Have the chef call other chefs. Ask them what coffee they are using for banquets. I bet you will find a better, more cost-effective alternative. Call your supplier and have them send in samples. Do the blind taste test. Always be looking at your top 20.

The other side of this is that your vendors work in reverse. They know what you buy in volume, and they look to increase your spending, not to decrease it. That is *their* game, so be better at that game than they are. They know who has their ducks in a row.

80/20 does not mean you ignore the food items that only account for 20% of your F&B revenues (which might be five hundred or more items). You continually look for better pricing and quality there too. Just do not lose sight of where the big opportunities are.

Watch a short video on the "80/20 Rule and Food Cost"

https://qrco.de/bd6XgA

Chapter 35

Top 10 Food Cost Controls

Food cost is a never-ending battle in a war that does not end. You can never take your foot off the gas, because if you do, you'll slow down, and when you slow down in the food-cost world it is expensive. Back in the day, I cut my teeth as a receiver, F&B cost control clerk and ultimately a F&B cost controller. Here is my top 10 list of food cost control strategies you can either put in place or re-commit to doing.

10. Shop Around

It sounds simple, and it is, but many hotels get complacent and don't keep their vendors on their toes. If you are buying the same products from the same vendors time and time again, you are overpaying. Make it a habit each month to shop 10% of your products, and remember the 80/20 rule.

9. Check Your Receiving

If someone is not meeting the truck and making sure that what's being delivered is what was ordered, then you are flying with your eyes closed. Companies know who does and who does not routinely check their deliveries. If you are on the wrong side of that equation, then your vendors may take advantage of you. Weight, actual product and quality can all suffer, and you are paying the price. Oh, and by the way—have a scale at the back door, make sure it is accurate and use it.

8.   Lock It Up

Food is right up there with cash and booze in your hotel's ecosystem. It needs to be under constant supervision, and when it is closing time you must lock it up. If you have a storage area that is away from the production area you must always lock it up. I cannot tell you how many times I have seen situations where food had developed legs.

7.   Menu Costings

Let's face it, people are busy and costing and re-costing a menu is time consuming. But having a menu that has not been costed at all, or which has not been costed lately, is an expensive mistake. Always be looking for price changes and reflect these in your costings. At the very least have these in an Excel spreadsheet and have the principal ingredient prices updated monthly. Test this one. Go to your kitchen today and ask the chef for his/her costings!

6.   Embrace Contribution Margin

It is one thing to have a good food cost percentage. But remember, we do not put percentages into the bank—we put dollars. Let me give you an example. We have two popular menu items: a salmon filet that costs $4 and sells for $20 (a 20% food cost), and we have a NY steak that costs $7 and sells for $26, a 27% food cost. Which is better for my food cost? That's the wrong question. The question is, which one has the highest contribution? Want to change your answer?

5.   Separation of Duties

In small hotels this is a challenge, and it may mean extra dollars to have someone other than the person who ordered the food receiving and checking it. However, it is essential to ensure the person ordering the items is not best friends with your supplier. I have seen this movie before. And another layer we want separated is to make sure the person ordering (whatever the item is—not just food) is not the one who writes the checks to pay for it.

4.   After Hours

The use of requisitions is critical, and the after-regular-storeroom-hours food issue is a vulnerable area to protect. Establish a procedure that requires more than one person to access the storeroom after hours. As an example, security or the night manager must accompany the kitchen personnel. Unfettered access to your lockups is an invitation too good for some to pass up.

3.   Invoice Approval

Food usually does not have an invoice included when it is delivered. It typically comes with only a packing slip. The invoice arrives later, usually by mail, and must be matched with the original packing slip. The best-in-class process here is to have these invoices and the accompanying packing slips reviewed and signed off on daily by the head chef. We want to see proof of delivery and inspection with the packing slip and the chef's approval for payment.

2.   Stock Rotation

Making sure that your food products are properly rotated takes more time, therefore some people do not do it. Make sure your operation is not one of those. Check to see the dates on items while stored. Oldest in the front – new stuff in the back. It might seem simple, but make sure you test it.

1. Waste

Measuring and controlling waste is very important. So important that you can even purchase a service that will help you monitor it. There is an acceptable amount of waste, given the fact that we are in the business of constructing menu items from raw ingredients. Make sure the waste gets monitored. Look in your trash on a regular basis and ask why this and that is getting tossed out. Over-production? Over-purchasing? And so on.

Being on top of your food cost is a never-ending job that requires you to be on your toes—and it pays off!

Watch a short video on "Understanding Food Cost"

https://qrco.de/bd7FCk

Chapter 36

Top 10 Beverage Cost Controls

Controlling the beverage cost is a big deal in hotels. People like to drink and that's great for the bar, but you have to remember the people serving your drinks need a tight set of checks and balances or else they may help themselves to your supplies. It's just human nature to mess around with the stuff at your fingertips all day long. There is a certain sense of entitlement as well because the wages are small, and people rely on tips. Bigger portions or the odd free one for a client can make a big difference in the tips left behind. Hotels have some special nuances, too, with multiple outlets, and with the beverages in lots of different locations, such as bars, restaurants, banquet rooms and storerooms.

Now, I'm not saying your beverage staff are stealing or anything like that, but what I *am* saying—and what this chapter is all about— is this: have a tight set of controls that you continuously monitor, and you will help the honest people stay that way while minimizing the actions of the mischievous.

From working the dining room and the bars in the early part of my career and a stint as a F&B Cost Controller, I learned a thing or two, and it's not rocket science. Rather, it is just good housekeeping and common sense. But like anything, if you don't practice it, it won't take care of itself. Put these controls in place and ensure they are followed every day, and you will keep more of what's yours.

Most of these controls work together to create a system you can utilize to organize your team's efforts and make the process of providing and selling alcohol in your hotel as efficient as possible.

10. Point of Sale First

Simply put, all sales must be recorded in the POS first. No ticket, no beverage. This ensures that the people on the floor must properly record the sale before the bartender makes the drink order. This separation of duty is critical for ensuring your waitstaff cannot get drink items prepared without first properly recording the sale. Skip this and you are wide open.

This is also an easy control to monitor: simply watch what's happening. Did Paul go from the customer's table to the POS and then to the bar? Did Susan grab the chit from the printer before she made the order for Paul?

9. Measuring Devices

All items dispensed must have a portion-controlling device. One of the best examples of this that already exists is bottled and draft beer. When we serve one of these it's already in the proper portion. A full glass of draft is what we expect and, other than over pours and foam, it is perfect. The same goes for the bottled beer. But spirits and wine are a different story. Ideally you want a computerized dispensing system for your spirits and house wine.

Today there is some excellent technology that allows you to measure individual staff performance around portion size poured versus the standard. With these systems you can reduce over-pouring by 2-4 percentage points of liquor or wine cost. A million dollars in liquor sales at a 20% cost when it really should be 17% is equal to $30,000, and it's an even greater cost with wine. But even without an automated system, you need to use measuring devices, such as jiggers for your alcohol and carafes for your wine.

8.   Voids and Adjustments

Closely controlling who has the authority to process credits inside your POS is a fundamental control point. However, it's often overlooked for efficiency. If a staff member who's serving your guests has the ability to adjust off the sale without someone else's approval, then you are wide open for fun and games to be played.

7.   The Need for a Separate Main Beverage Storeroom

In hotels we have multiple outlets and we want to ensure we control the inventory with a central distribution and location. In this case, it's obvious that volume matters, and you will want to ensure you have enough—but don't assume you can take a shortcut. Without a central storeroom and someone managing the inventory and its distribution, you are not going to be able to establish sufficient control.

6.   Separate Ordering, Approval and Receiving

Separating the functions and the people who perform them is critical. In full-service hotels the order should be prepared by the storeroom staff based on their minimum/maximum par stock for the storeroom as well as the special banquet wine requirements. The order then must be approved by the F&B or Operations Manager. Once approved the order is placed by the storeroom clerk, and when it's delivered or picked up, depending upon the set up, it must be verified by the hotel receiver.

Someone independent of the storeroom and the operation must verify the order received. It's ideal if that someone reports to the financial department. Create the same separation for your food and all other operating supplies for all departments.

5.   Outlet Par Stocks

Establishing individual outlet par stocks for liquor, beer and wine ensures that you have an inventory framework in which to work. The par stocks should be set up for all outlets except for Banquets. Banquet volumes and customer-specific events preclude the par stock practicality for banquets.

For the rest of your outlets par stock is how many bottles of each item that there should be on hand, full or empty. This system allows you to know the maximum dollar value of inventory on hand for each outlet. This is very helpful when it comes time for inventory to know what the expected range of the dollar value of inventory is as well as how many bottles of each individual item you expect to count.

4.   Liquor and Wine Bottle Stickers

With an established individual par stock for each outlet, the next part of the system is stickers. From the storeroom, all liquor and wine products require stickers to be affixed to each bottle, with a different color sticker used for each outlet. Take the time to set this up. Order your stickers so they are sequentially numbered and make sure you have a constant supply. This will cost you a few hundred dollars per year, but the stickers are worth their weight in gold.

Why? When you spot check a bar or do your inventory, every sticker should be the same color. This ensures the products you have issued end up in the right bar. This also ensures staff can't bring in their own bottles (to sell and keep the cash). If they do, they won't have the proper sticker. Keep an eye on the trash with this control as a bottle in the garbage without a sticker is a smoking gun.

3.   Requisitions

Require the use of requisitions for absolutely everything issued to all outlets. Use different requisitions for each outlet based on the individual par stock. Have these requisitions pre-printed and sequentially numbered. Part of the closing duties is to submit a daily requisition for all items required to bring the bar back to its par stock.

2.   Bottle for Bottle Exchange

Part of the opening duties for each bar is the retrieval of the order placed the prior evening at the end of the shift. Part of the receiving of the order from the storeroom is the exchange of the empty bottle for a full one. The storeroom clerk must ensure all stickers match the outlet's color and that all empty bottles are counted and add up to the requested order. The final step is to deface the sticker so it cannot be used again.

The bottle-for-bottle exchange is critical for maintaining the par stock and ensuring the outlet has the proper supplies to meet business and customer requirements.

1.   Transfer Slips

Beverages need to move around your hotel in order to ensure your par stocks are efficient and not too high. With multiple outlets and expensive, slow-moving items like liquors and fine spirits, you will want to only have one bottle on hand in the key outlets. When the bar runs out of one of these items and the customer wants more, they need the ability to transfer stock from one outlet to the other, and the transfer slips explain why this is being done.

If you see opportunities to introduce these types of controls, then you need to get cracking. Without this framework, evaporation is certain!

V

HOTEL BUSINESS STRATEGY AND FINANCIAL ANALYSIS

The hotel business is not terribly technical but there are some basic financial strategies that you need to understand. In this section I examine some of the common ones you need to be fluent with, and I share some budgeting knowledge.

Chapter 37

Understanding REVPAR and REVPAR Index

REVPAR and the **REVPAR index** are different, and I'm going to explain them both in this chapter. Understanding REVPAR and the REVPAR index is the beginning point for understanding what's going on at a hotel. It's the most important piece of the puzzle from a revenue point of view.

REVPAR

REVPAR stands for "revenue per available room." It is a cornerstone metric of the hotel world, and rightfully so. It is the product of occupancy times rate, as shown in this simple formula:

Occupancy x Rate = REVPAR

Here's an example: If my hotel was 60% occupied last night and my average rate was $100.00, my REVPAR would be $60.00 (100.00 x .6).

The other way to calculate this would be to take the total rooms in my hotel—in this example it is 500—and divide that by the total room revenue from the previous night. At 60% that means I had 300 rooms occupied, and I will multiply that by $100 to get my room revenue:

$$300 \times 100 = \$30,000$$

To calculate the REVPAR, I divide the room revenue by the rooms available:

$$\$30,000/500 = \$60$$

I can calculate the REVPAR for any period—a week, month, or year—the same way.

REVPAR calculations are relatively new in the hospitality industry. I do not want to draw too much attention to my age here, but when I went to hotel school, REVPAR was not on the menu. The key figures we put together involved the occupancy and average room rates. Knowing these numbers is important, but simply having the data for occupancy and rate only helps create a part of the picture. REVPAR is a more sophisticated measurement that combines occupancy and rate into a single number that's more meaningful than either is alone. It allows us to see the entire picture using one metric.

REVPAR Index

The REVPAR index takes an individual hotel's REVPAR and compares it to the REVPAR of other comparably competitive hotels. It shows you where you are relative to your competition in an index, which allows you to see the variance expressed in hotels of the same relative size and service level, and also shows you how much better or worse you're performing in the competitive set (CompSet).

In the days before STR's REVPAR index, we would do a call around to find out what the other hotels in our city were doing each month for occupancy and rate. I think a lot of us thought some hotels fabricated their results.

Then somewhere around the mid-1990s a company called STR—Smith Travel Research—started a business based on capturing and sharing occupancy, rate and REVPAR for various hotels. They sold a subscription to this data. Now you can more clearly and quickly see how well you are doing versus your competitors. It's more likely too that the data that's collected *en masse* in this fashion is less "massaged" than it once might have been.

There are three reasons why it's useful to calculate the REVPAR index.

- It allows you to **see how well you're executing** your sales and revenue management strategies relative to your competition. Given the current product you have, how well are you selling the hotel?
- The index **shows you what your variance is** relative to your competitors, and what that gap is worth. Let's say your index is 15% below the set. This means that with a potential investment in your product you could close or beat that gap, and that translates into potential dollars of profit to justify your investment.
- The index helps you to be continually **aware of how your hotel is positioned** relative to its competitors, so you can see if your rate and occupancy strategies are working. For example, maybe you want to lead on rate (have the highest rate in the area), because you feel in the long run this is the best game plan for your asset; the index will enlighten you as to the potential impact of this strategy.

Calculating REVPAR Index

Choosing a competitive set of hotels to compare can be difficult, and it needs to make sense. You can't compare hotels that charge $50 a night versus hotels that charge $150 and up. If you are in a busy city setting, sorting this out can be easier because you'll have more hotels to choose from. If you are in a resort setting, look at hotels that are similar in product and service to yours. Once you choose your set, you are not going to want to change it unless there are very good reasons to do so—such as a new hotel in your marketplace.

Having a positive index (above 100%) is where you want to be. The bigger, the better.

In many HMAs (hotel management agreements) having and maintaining a positive index is an important test. In some HMAs the manager is required to maintain a positive index or they can lose the contract to manage the hotel. This can be a costly problem for the management company, because losing the flag means you just lost all the fees you collect from that hotel. You might even find yourself in a situation where you have to make up the lost profit and pay it to the owner.

Looking Across the Top of the Chart

We start with each hotel's "Room Base"—the number of rooms in each hotel.

We then multiply the number of rooms by the days in the month to get Total Rooms Available.

Next, we enter the actual Rooms Occupied for the month, followed next by the percentage of occupancy for this month for each hotel.

Following those are the potential and actual share based on occupancy. This is the first point where we see the individual performance of the properties in relative terms, only on occupancy to their competitors. This is also known as the MPI: market penetration index.

This produces the net capture index.

The next step is to add the monthly average rate—ARI: average rate index—which produces the property room revenue in the column on the far right.

Once we have the room revenue, we can calculate the individual hotel REVPAR.

Once you have the REVPAR, divide it by the overall REVPAR of the sample set to produce the REVPAR index, also known as the RGI: revenue generating index.

Hotel Set	Room Base	Total Rms Available	Rooms Occupied	Occupancy Percent	Market Share Potential	Market Share Actual	Net Cap Index MPI	Average Rate	ARI	REVPAR	REVPAR Index RGI	Total Room Revenue
Hotel 1	400	12400	9325	75.2%	17.1%	17.2%	100.8%	$145.50	95.1%	$109.42	95.9%	$1,356,788
Hotel 2	325	10075	6875	68.2%	13.9%	12.7%	91.5%	$165.23	108.0%	$112.75	98.8%	$1,135,956
Hotel 3	450	13950	11005	78.9%	19.2%	20.3%	105.8%	$163.45	106.9%	$128.94	113.0%	$1,798,767
Hotel 4	375	11625	8741	75.2%	16.0%	16.1%	100.8%	$159.24	104.1%	$119.73	105.0%	$1,391,917
Hotel 5	500	15500	10789	69.6%	21.3%	19.9%	93.3%	$145.85	95.4%	$101.52	89.0%	$1,573,576
Hotel 6	295	9145	7487	81.9%	12.6%	13.8%	109.8%	$138.45	90.5%	$113.35	99.4%	$1,036,575
Total Set	2345	72695	54222	74.6%	100.0%	100.0%	100.0%	$152.96	100.0%	$114.09	100.0%	$8,293,579

REVPAR index calculation

That might seem like a lot of math but it's really a simple set of calculations—and ultimately it's a worthwhile endeavor in terms of understanding these key metrics of hotel operations.

Watch a short video that explains "REVPAR Index"

https://qrco.de/bd6Xj8

Chapter 38

Why Your Hotel Needs a Daily Pick-up Report

Y ou might be reading this and saying to yourself, "Well, for sure every hotel needs a daily pick-up report"—a record of rooms sold from one day to the next. But I bet you would be surprised how many hotels either do not use their pick-up report, or do not use it properly. They are missing the excellent financial opportunity that arises whenever the daily pick-up report is managed with a good strategy.

I have never and will never profess to being any kind of expert at hotel revenue management; that's an ever-expanding field of specialization within the hotel business. I see myself strictly as a novice in that arena. The purpose of this chapter is to point out how to use the daily pick-up report to inspire and invigorate your leadership team around the financial aspects of your business. Every day in your hotel you need to beat the drums of great guest service, superior colleague engagement and nonstop financial leadership, and the pick-up report is the magic stick-to-the-money focus—the most important tool to look at every day and the engine that drives the hotel.

Everything in your hotel operationally revolves around the occupancy (how many rooms you have) plus the arrivals and departures. This information offers a direct insight into how busy you are going to be. The rates and REVPAR are critical elements, but for most of your managers it is the occupancy that they and you pay the closest attention to.

Most hotels start their month with about half of their occupancy on the books. The pace at which you fill is the critical plot line, and the financial story is written each month based on the peaks and valleys of this journey. Having a laser focus on the pick-up is what guides good managers to better staffing and expense-planning decisions.

The focus on the daily pick-up report in the month is the daily build, and we adjust rates for future dates based on last-minute demand.

The star of the morning meeting should always be the fresh, hot-off-the-press daily pick-up report. The day-by-day occupancy for the next 1, 2, 3 days and the week ahead is critical for your operations people to zero in on. From these cues come the questions and answers that drive incremental decision making with your leadership teams.

> **Pro Tip:** For a good morning meeting, ensure that a paper copy of the daily projected occupancy gets distributed each day, and that you religiously execute a thorough review of the day's critical numbers. Eyeballs on the page equals action with the schedule. No autopilot, please.

If the occupancy for tomorrow is now 10 rooms less than it was two days ago, this means a shift must be removed in housekeeping, or an eight-hour shift is now four hours. Same for arrivals and departures. The same philosophy applies to the desk and the outlets. Watching these critical barometers means your managers are adjusting and fine-tuning their landing plans.

If the occupancy for tomorrow is now five more rooms than it was yesterday, then how are you going to manage turning the house with the same labor you had previously planned? Train your managers to schedule for less, not more—that is, it's usually best if you can figure out a way to get the job done even though you have fewer employees present, than it is to have more staff on hand than truly necessary.

Ensure each operational leader is adjusting schedules based on the daily occupancy. If you are cruising along at 30,000 feet with the same number of bodies and hours worked regardless of the daily needs, then no one is watching the switch. Critical areas like the front desk, housekeeping and the F&B outlets need to be measuring daily productivity using their schedules to capture projected results.

If you sit in neutral, the labor train will run you over. Be on top of the scheduling decisions each and every day. For many managers this is exactly how they play and win. But for others they just set it and forget it. They publish the schedule, and that's that—no creative review of the critical aspects of the single biggest cost: payroll.

The hotel business is a game of inches. A couple of extra employee hours here and a couple there and before you know it, it all adds up to cost you a bundle. Use the discussion around the daily pick-up report to check in with your departmental teams. Ask them what their projected productivity is this week. Remind them to tell you what it was last week and what their forecasted result for the month is. Do this with a kind and curious manner, all the while patiently insisting that each key member knows and manages their labor with the proper tools to help them and you succeed.

Depending upon the size of your hotel, these incremental adjustments add up to a whole lot of dough. This pie can be going out the door in the form of inefficient scheduling or it can accrue positively to your bottom line. It is all up to you and the leadership direction you create.

Using your daily pick-up report effectively is the most important tool you have to foster the proper hospitality financial leadership culture in your hotel.

Watch a short video on "Daily Rooms Pick-up Report"

https://qrco.de/bd6X2o

Chapter 39

Fixed and Variable Costs and Room Revenue Management

I have spoken to many revenue managers who have told me how much their cost is to take a room, to make the last sale of the day. What I hear concerns me because it tells me some people do not understand the fixed versus variable components of payroll and expenses in their hotels. We'll break this out more below, but in short, fixed costs are what doesn't change regardless of whether or not a room is sold: cable TV, front-desk services, and so on. Variable costs include room-cleaning costs, among other things. Understanding the various costs involved can help determine the value of reducing the standard room rate in order to book the room and still make a profit.

The other day I was on the phone with Bob, a revenue manager at a New York City hotel. He told me his cost to take a room in his hotel in NYC was $290.

"What?" I exclaimed over the telephone.

"Yes, that's the cost."

To which I replied, "That's the total cost of all your expenses, both fixed and variable?" Silence ensued for a moment, then I said, "Let's slow things down and look at the scenario."

Let's say it's noon and you have 10 rooms left to sell for the day. The demand for today has been strong but in the last week we have been up and down around the +10 mark. My question is, "Exactly what does it cost you in variable expenses to sell those last 10 rooms, and how should they be priced?"

This is a very different question than: "What are costs per room occupied?"

The fixed expenses in a hotel are many. Let's say we are running a house count of 285 rooms and occupancy of 96.6%. All the costs for the following under this scenario are fixed. In other words—and this is the pivot point—it will cost no additional dollars on any of the following items to take those last 10 rooms:

- Front desk, guest services, reservations payroll
- Cable television
- Contract services
- Linen and uniform purchases
- Equipment purchase
- Decorations
- All overhead expenses and payroll
- All owner expenses

The truly variable expenses are:

- Room attendant payroll and benefits
- Linen cleaning
- Guest supplies
- Paper supplies
- Cleaning supplies
- Travel agent commissions
- Reservation fees
- Credit card commissions
- Brand fees
- Energy (some variable)

Semi-variable expenses include things like energy; for example, we have to have heat, light and power an occupied room, but we are also already paying an electricity bill for the hotel.

Let's look at the chart below for a summary:

Variable expenses on a $200 same-day room price	
Room attendant pay (30 min x $24 per hour)	$12.00
Variable employee benefits ($12 x 25%)	$3.00
Linen cleaning – per room occupied cost	$2.25
Guest supplies – per room occupied cost	$3.60
Paper supplies – per room occupied cost	$0.50
Cleaning supplies – per room occupied cost	$1.40
Travel agent commissions – used an OTA @ 18%	$36.00
Credit card commissions 3%	$6.00
Brand fees 7%	$14.00
Energy costs (some) (room vs. building) (25% of $17)	$4.25
Total variable cost	$83.00
Incremental profit	$117.00

So if we assume a regular room price of $290 but sell that room at $200 for a same-day price, the chart clearly shows the individual costs for the variable items and the incremental profit from the sale of each room. For an annual picture let's look at the impact on profits if the hotel was able to sell these 10 rooms half the days of the year: (180 days x 10 rooms x $117) = $210,600 in additional profit that goes straight to the bottom line

This boosts the NOP (net operating profit) closer to 10%. The real impact is an additional profit of $210K, which adds an additional $2.6 million in asset value using a very modest capitalization rate of 8:

(8/100 = 12.5), therefore 12.5 x 210,600 = $2,632,500

When you think about your current selling policy as it relates to last-minute inventory, make sure you have a good handle on the real variable costs to sell those last-minute rooms. Don't be confused by the big fixed cost per room stickers.

Know there is a balance between building the base, yielding the inventory in the largest demand period, and selling those last rooms more often.

Chapter 40

Understanding Flow Thru

I use the abbreviation "flow thru" as a catch-all phrase to describe how much money flows from revenue to profit when comparing the current period to a like earlier period (for example, July this year to July last year, and/or year-to-date July this year to year-to-date July last year). Another term to describe this measurement is "retention."

A good analogy to grasp this concept is your paycheck. If I give you a raise of $1000 per week, how much of this $1000 will you personally retain (your profit), and how much will get eaten up by higher taxes and other deductions?

The same goes for additional revenues in your hotel. If revenues are $50,000 higher this month than, say, the same month last year, how much of that $50,000 will flow thru to the profit line? It's great to increase the rate and overall revenues in a hotel, but what the owner will really want to know is how much of that increase he or she will actually keep in profits.

Understanding flow thru is key for understanding the overall profit model of your hotel. Revenues go up and down in different departments. Measuring flow thru by department and by the key drivers is the basis for understanding your hotel's real financial results—and most importantly its financial potential. Here are some questions to get your flow thru imagination going.

- The overall revenues year-to-date are up by 1.3 million dollars compared to last year. How much should flow thru to Gross Operating Profit (GOP; revenue minus operating expenses)?
- Occupancy is up over last year by 5% and, at the same time, rates have increased by $15/night and room revenues are up $720,000. How much of this increase should flow thru into both room profit and GOP?
- In the Restaurant Department, the average check is up by $2, and as a result food revenues are up $10,000. How much should flow thru into F&B profit and GOP?
- Liquor revenues are up over last year in my lounge by $7,000. How much should flow thru into F&B profit and GOP?
- Banquet food sales are $50,000 higher this month than the same month last year, driven by both higher volume and higher average checks. How much should flow thru into the F&B profit and GOP?

The way we calculate flow thru is straightforward:

1. Subtract the revenues from two like periods (different years)—the current period minus the previous one.
2. Subtract the profit from the same two periods.
3. Divide the difference in profit by the difference in the revenue.

See the sample chart below:

	2022 Actual	2019 Actual	Variance	
Total Revenues	2,478,978 =	2,312,064 -	166,914	
			/	
GOP	292,500 =	273,919 -	18,581	11.1% Flow

All the revenue streams in your hotel have two attributes: *pricing* and *volume*. Pricing is the average room rate or average cover; volume is rooms sold or covers served. Understanding the difference and measuring the impact is the key to understanding and measuring departmental flow thru.

Measuring flow thru to the prior period is normally a stronger comparison than measuring flow thru to budget or forecast. This is because when we compare the flow thru from one real period to another real period it is more of an apples-to-apples comparison. When we compare flow thru to the budget, we are comparing a real result to a projection.

A word of caution: when comparing the flow thru from one period to another it is important to include any events that may have had an impact on the results. This is where a good memory and a great monthly property commentary come into play. Let's say that last year in the month of May we had a great group month because of a city-wide event. That fact will artificially skew the flow thru in the current month of May. Searching in your departments for the "problem" as to why your revenue is so much lower this May than last May will be a waste of time. So being able to articulate the impact of past and current events is very important.

Negative flow thru is also an important concept and calculation to master. When revenues decrease, we want to be able to mitigate the impact this has on the profit lines. We want to be able to minimize the profit loss, to see where we can cut expenses and so retain a level of profit that is much less than the drop in revenue. A target to aim for is negative 50% flow thru. Example: revenues this March are down by $100,000 to March last year. Our negative flow thru target should be no more than a negative $50,000 drop in GOP. If we are asleep at the switch, we could easily lose the full $100,000 or more.[5]

---

[5] To explore flow thru more, I invite you to search via the "blog" tab on my website, www.hotelfinancialcoach.com. Enter "flow" in the search box and you should quickly find three articles on flow thru that will give you additional information. And if you're really serious about understanding

ADDITIONAL REVENUE FLOW THRU
(THEORETICAL FLOW THRU TARGETS)

Room Rate **90%**

Room Occupancy **80%**

F&B Banquets **50%**

F&B Outlets **25%**

Over-heads **-20%**

—— *Increase in Revenue* → % Target for Profit

Rooms Flow thru

Rate increases

The Rooms Department is the engine in 99% of the hotels in the world. The greatest contributor to performance is rate, followed by occupancy. If my rate is up $10 over the same month last year and I sell the same number of rooms—let's say 18,500—my room revenue just went up by $185,000.

The question is: How much of this increased revenue should I be able to keep as profit?

What we need to examine is whether there were additional costs associated with our increase in rate. In point of fact, very little else needs to go up when my rate grows. Depending on various factors, I

---

flow thru calculations, send me a note and request my flow-thru cheat sheet.

may need to spend some of this increased revenue on third-party commissions. I may also need to spend more on my reservation expense from my brand. This is because the commissions and fees to the brand are all based on the volume of sales dollars—more revenue directly impacts the expenses.

Other than these cursory items no additional expense or payroll in the Rooms Department need to be spent, because all we have done is raise the rate.

Other costs that will be impacted by the increased revenues are credit card commissions, centralized fees, and management fees. A good rule of thumb is that I should see 90% of any additional revenue flow thru in rooms profit and 85% in GOP as a result of the increased room rate.

Your hotel manager may take it upon herself to spend a little more that month to catch up on some cleaning or other expenses based on the increased revenue, but this is not directly related to the increase in rate.

Occupancy increases

Let's say my hotel this month saw an increase of six points in occupancy over the same month last year. This resulted in an additional 300 rooms sold and an additional $45,000 in room revenue. How much should flow thru to profit?

With occupancy versus rate increases, this question is a bit more complicated.

Every time I sell a room I have both fixed and variable expenses associated with the sale. While the increase will not require significant additional resources at the front desk, in reservations or guest services, it will necessitate additional room attendants and housekeeping labor. I will consume more amenities, laundry, guest supplies and probably should pay higher commissions to third parties and more in reservation expenses to my brand (because the commissions and fees are based on the volume of sales dollars—more revenue directly impacts these expenses). I will also pay higher credit card commissions, centralized fees, and management fees. So, as a rule of thumb, from increased occupancy I should see 85% as increased rooms profit and 80% in increased GOP.

Food & Beverages Flow Thru

In the food and beverage department, we need to have a much bigger calculator to assess flow thru.

For one thing, profitability characteristics are very different between food sales and beverage sales.

Within food sales it is key to distinguish the profitability of all the different meal periods, as well as the relationship between outlet sales (bars and restaurants) versus banquets.

What would you rather have: revenue increases from dinner or from coffee breaks? Increases in outlet sales or banquets? Which would have a bigger impact on profit?

With beverage sales, the profit margins for liquor, beer, and wine need to be understood, as do the dynamics between outlets versus banquets.

When we look at the average customer price for food, we also need to consider the contribution margin. It is nice to see the average cover increase, but what profit do I make from the different types of sales inside my F&B operation?

All of this looks complicated on the surface, but it is generally simpler than it appears. With a little analysis and some patience, we can build a model that will help us see the optimal picture for profitability in our F&B operation. With this picture, we can strive to create the optimal recipe for F&B success.

That is the key: Understanding what the optimal mix is and getting our sales and conference services people selling *that*. Getting our outlet managers and servers to understand what items have the biggest contribution to profit and have them sell accordingly. If we were selling cars, we would want to know which model generates the biggest margin, and the accessories that drive profits. Our business is no different. Flow thru is at the heart of understanding this profit model.

Minor Operating and Non-operating Department Flow Thru

The same principles apply for spa, golf and retail operations.

In this case, non-operating department flow thru is an important factor to monitor. I cannot tell you how many statements I see where there is a nice increase in the top-line revenues but most of the potential profits are chewed up by non-operating departmental creep.

Administration costs, sales and marketing and maintenance flow thru need to be measured and managed. If you cannot readily see this, you are missing a powerful tool.

Conclusion

Creating the flow thru measurements in your financials is a relatively straightforward process. All you need to do is to pull out the numbers you want to see, like the change in revenue and the change in profit from two different periods, and divide the two. Display these on your financials and you will have a whole new understanding of your business and be much more effective in your ability to hold others to account for managing their departmental flow thru.

Mastering flow thru is the key to hotel profit maximization.

Understand where you are winning, and point your team, sellers and operators in that direction.

Watch a short video on "Understanding Flow Thru"

https://qrco.de/bd6Z71

Chapter 41

The Six Elements of GOPPAR

GOPPAR, or "gross operating profit per available room," is the new and exciting measurement everyone is talking about in the hotel business. Why, you ask? As we all know, COVID kicked us hard, and overnight our focus went from REVPAR to profit, and the lesson in that was this: we don't take revenue to the bank, we take profits.

But let's be honest. It is a bit of a stretch to comprehend. It is a little more complicated than REVPAR. Why, you ask? Well, REVPAR has two components: occupancy and rate. That's all you need to square the calculation. GOPPAR has six components and I am going to lay them all out here.

A big part of the struggle people have is the idea that GOPPAR is an accounting thing. Now, while it's true that the calculation is based on accounting theory, stick with me; it is really a straightforward concept. GOPPAR, like REVPAR, is easy to square. You just have six pieces to deal with instead of only two. The six pieces are groups of like items:

1. Room Revenues – REVPAR
2. F&B Revenues – FBRPAR
3. Other Hotel Revenues – OTRPAR
4. Hotel Cost of Goods Sold – CGSPAR
5. Hotel Payroll – PAYPAR
6. Hotel Expenses – EXPPAR

Six Elements of GOPPAR

REVPAR+FBRPAR+OTRPAR+CGSPAR+PAYPAR+EXPPAR=GOPPAR

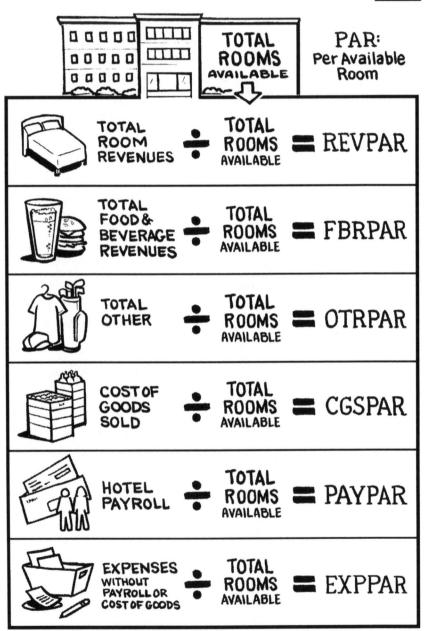

TOTAL ROOMS AVAILABLE

PAR:
Per Available Room

TOTAL ROOM REVENUES	÷	TOTAL ROOMS AVAILABLE	= REVPAR
TOTAL FOOD & BEVERAGE REVENUES	÷	TOTAL ROOMS AVAILABLE	= FBRPAR
TOTAL OTHER	÷	TOTAL ROOMS AVAILABLE	= OTRPAR
COST OF GOODS SOLD	÷	TOTAL ROOMS AVAILABLE	= CGSPAR
HOTEL PAYROLL	÷	TOTAL ROOMS AVAILABLE	= PAYPAR
EXPENSES WITHOUT PAYROLL OR COST OF GOODS	÷	TOTAL ROOMS AVAILABLE	= EXPPAR

The way the accounting system works allows us to group these six items together, because each account is recorded separately. If we have all the amounts from each of these six items and the hotel follows the *Uniform System of Accounts for the Lodging Industry*—"USALI" (You Sally)—then we have absolutely every dollar captured, and we simply divide the total amount from each group by the same available rooms. These six items equal the hotel's GOP every time, in every hotel.

There are no other items that we need to consider so long as we follow You Sally.

I am going to define and give you an example of each of the six components just so we are clear. Remember, we just divide each by the total rooms available for the same corresponding period.

REVPAR – Total room revenues divided by total rooms available for any period, typically for a day, a month or a year. Does not include no-show or attrition.

FBRPAR – Total F&B revenues divided by total rooms available for any period, typically for a day, a month or a year. Includes all other F&B revenue items, including food, liquor, beer, wine, minerals, banquet room rentals, cover charges, audio visual, pass throughs, house portion of gratuities, rentals, electricity, and any other item that sold to a guest in the F&B outlets and banquets.

OTRPAR – Total Other revenues divided by total rooms available for any period, typically for a day, a month or a year. Includes all minor operating departments and other income. Basically, any income the hotel receives that is not derived from rooms or F&B. Typical items like telephones, SPA, golf, health clubs, shops, rents, concessions, interest income, no-shows, attrition and foreign exchange.

CGSPAR – The total cost of goods sold from all applicable departments divided by total rooms available for any period, typically for a day, a month or a year. Cost of goods derived from food and beverage sales make up most of the dollars here, but we also must include any other minor operating departments cost of sales. The rooms department does not have a cost of goods sold, just expenses. Why, you may ask? Because Sally says so.

PAYPAR – Total hotel payroll for all employees in all departments divided by total rooms available for any period, typically for a day, a month or a year. Includes all payroll items including wages, benefits, supplemental and payroll taxes. Does not include payroll processing fees. Those are an expense.

EXPPAR – Total expenses divided by total rooms available for any period, typically for a day, a month or a year. Includes all expenses from all departments including energy. Does not include any payroll or cost of goods items. It does not include financial expenses like insurance and property taxes. These are recorded below GOP, so they are not part of the GOPPAR calculation.

With these six items grouped into their own separate boxes we encompass everything that makes up a hotel's GOP.

Watch a short video on "GOPPAR"

https://qrco.de/bdbUvw

Chapter 42

What's the Only Thing We Know for Sure About the Budget?

The budget is a BIG deal; it consumes so much time and energy in the hotel. Getting it right is a critical element of any branded, managed hotel. If you are reading this and you do not prepare an annual budget, you are probably scratching your head and wondering what I am talking about.

In your average hotel the budget process is a two- to three-month deal. It means—or it *should* mean—that each key manager is implicated in doing their part by preparing and negotiating the payroll and expenses for the department they manage.

The annual gut-wrenching process we call creating a budget can be, to put it politely a "Caca Show." But it need not be. That is the scoop with this chapter. Because as we've said frequently in this book, the only thing we know for sure about the budget is this: it's wrong. That's right. It's wrong every time. It will never be the correct answer.

So why do we put so much time and effort into preparing it?

Hotel budgeting and forecasting is not like grade 10 algebra. There is no correct answer for our problem. Either the budget is too big or too small. We will either beat it or it will have us for lunch. No one ever just makes their budget. The budget, properly viewed, is a set of guidelines to follow, the minimum requirements for our operation given different levels of busy-ness.

So, with this revelation clearly called out, why do we put so much effort and angst into the annual preparation of this beast? Most managers spend an inordinate amount of time and sweat preparing their piece. They typically shoot for the stars with the items they include while knowing in the back of their minds that their wish list of additional staff and expenses is going to be shot down at first light. They want to right all the wrongs and finally get what they need to properly run their department, or so they think. A typical rookie move. A valiant thought and a noble quest, but it always ends the same: you are getting less to do more next year.

A much more practical and realistic approach is needed here.

Let's say we are looking at 2022 and preparing a budget for 2023. What were the parameters in 2022: revenues, rate, occupancy, REVPAR, payroll and expenses? We plan our budget for 2023 to reflect the results of 2022, plus or minus 5%. Having a look at that "benchmark" year could help us plan a "top-level" report that gives each key manager a target to plan their budget around. Why try to reinvent the wheel?

A budget is simply a business plan with numbers. As the old saying goes, "Any road will take you where you want to go when you are travelling without a map." What you need from the budget are the parameters you can operate within. For example, what were/are your payroll and expenses given different levels of REVPAR? You will notice I did not say occupancy; I said REVPAR. How much revenue coming in equals the amount of resources needed to deliver a great guest experience? In the end, that is all we are trying to achieve. Simply put a plan in place that tells us where we are going and what we will need to get to our destination.

All the while we need to remember that only thing we know for sure about the budget is that it's wrong! It is a great document, but it is only a planning exercise, and if properly designed it creates a roadmap to follow. Once we get the budget done and approved, we move into the year it's written for. Then we do our monthly forecasts. This is where the planning gets real.

Watch a short video on "The Only Thing We Know for sure About the Hotel Budget"

https://qrco.de/bd6XS6

Chapter 43

Why Managing Your Budget Is Like Playing Baseball

If you're involved in the budget in your hotel and you've also played baseball then you are probably saying to yourself that I am off my rocker for drawing a connection between the two. The budget is a mean, unruly and nasty guest that comes to visit every year and which sometimes doesn't leave (get completed) for weeks, even months. And working with a budget is certainly not fun and engaging in the way a good game of baseball can be.

But there's more than one way to look at a budget. So, let's dig a little deeper and see what I'm talking about. Much of life is how we choose to do battle—managing the budget in your hotel is no different.

To start with we need to recognize the budget for what it is: a business plan with numbers. Our job is to beat it at its own game. It's important to remember you'll never win all the games you play but with some creative strategies you are going to be better equipped to win more often, and that's what I'll share here.

The first thing to do is get comfortable with the basic rules of baseball and hotel budget-making. The first basic rule is there are at least nine innings in a baseball game, and in the hotel financial/budget-making world there are 12 innings—months—to play.

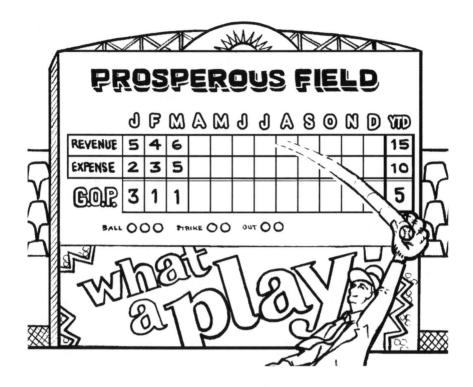

Those 12 months represent 12 opportunities to win, and even if you lose some innings, you'll still have the opportunity to catch up, especially if you fall behind in the earlier rounds. To bring this strategy to life, you need a system to follow. We need to have a 1-2-3 financial strategy up and running in our hotel.

1. Do monthly financial statements using the accrual basis.
2. Incorporate a current, detailed year-end monthly rolling forecast.
3. Most importantly, include all department managers in the monthly forecast and reforecast process. Without their involvement and commitment, you are sunk.

No sense getting bent out of shape when you fail to deliver on any month, or even suffer a string of defeats, because you have a couple of months where you can literally hit it out of the park and not only catch up but pull into the lead.

	Jan '23 ACTUAL	Feb '23 ACTUAL	Mar '23 ACTUAL	Apr '23 FORECAST	May '23 FORECAST	June '23 FORECAST	July '23 FORECAST	Aug '23 FORECAST	Sept '23 BUDGET	Oct '23 BUDGET	Nov '23 BUDGET	Dec '23 BUDGET	Total ACT/FCST	Total BUDGET
Total REVPAR	$ 113.58	$ 144.97	$ 181.19	$ 216.37	$ 294.00	$ 375.27	$ 256.94	$ 281.64	$ 301.37	$ 318.82	$ 239.65	$ 141.77	$ 239.08	$ 242.76
Total Operating Rev.	880,249	1,014,815	1,404,219	1,622,745	2,278,491	2,814,549	1,991,306	2,182,717	2,260,308	2,470,851	1,992,345	1,323,112	17,324,512	18,211,423
DEPARTMENTAL PROFIT														
Rooms	234,223	334,082	553,636	724,795	1,194,218	1,561,150	884,043	1,024,628	1,175,935	1,300,411	898,719	335,987	10,221,828	10,665,234
Food & Bev.	(79,532)	(27,778)	53,388	(2,676)	83,336	131,547	23,848	62,241	87,845	98,395	47,624	(5,884)	472,353	675,321
Other Depts.	25,863	(1,255)	(10,647)	9,974	6,745	15,460	15,716	14,983	9,125	23,433	13,703	6,370	129,471	128,456
Total Departmental Profit	180,554	305,049	596,377	732,094	1,284,299	1,708,157	923,607	1,101,852	1,277,906	1,422,239	960,045	336,473	10,823,651	11,469,011
Total Undistributed Expenses	530,287	504,158	552,981	577,377	587,046	641,109	658,407	601,136	684,084	634,146	612,312	534,511	7,117,554	6,999,876
Gross Operating Profit	(349,733)	(199,109)	43,396	154,717	697,253	1,067,047	265,199	500,716	588,822	788,093	397,224	(198,038)	3,706,097	3,896,756
Earnings Before Interest, Taxes, Depreciation	(454,439)	(303,786)	(82,284)	31,373	603,500	916,628	131,752	363,130	450,692	645,035	268,426	(56,789)	2,513,238	2,743,243
Replacement Reserve	17,568	20,177	61,053	48,532	68,685	84,436	59,739	65,480	67,809	74,127	53,921	32,961	654,490	650,112
EBITDA Less Replacement Reserve	($472,008)	($323,964)	($143,337)	($17,160)	$534,816	$832,192	$ 72,013	$297,650	$382,883	$570,908	$214,505	($ 89,750)	$1,858,748	$1,925,435

In this example we have the actual for the first three months of 2021. And you can see by looking at, say, the GOP for these months that things did not go according to the budget. But at this point you can reel the year-end performance back in by working a re-forecast in any month up to the end of the year.

The process goes like this: first actualize the current month, then do a detailed forecast of 30, 60, 90 days and finally a year-end target. This is where you need to do everything possible to make sure the entire team is focused on the year-end result. That means you need to have a team that knows where all the bodies are buried and how you can find the savings in payroll and expenses to drive the profit back into positive territory. That is the game you play. You can really benefit from realizing the game is not over just because you are behind.

Another critical element is your revenue management strategy. As you can see in the table above, you are behind in REVPAR compared to the budget. In this situation, move heaven and earth to find your way back to the target. Just because you fell down in the first quarter does not mean you do not have a fighting chance to turn the ship around.

I cannot tell you how many years I had to battle back from early innings where we were getting our butts kicked financially. Falling behind on the revenues and spending more than planned. But the key is always: don't give up, do not throw in the towel.

Why? Because just like baseball, you can have a great inning (or three, or six) and find yourself magically back in business. The bad luck and seemingly dead market and economy that delivered you such a thrashing in the early innings can turn on a dime.

That is why managing your hotel budget is just like playing baseball. You have several innings to play and win and, most importantly, you never give up! Your next grand slam is just around the corner, and hitting it out of the park is entirely possible as long as you are keeping score—every month!

Watch a short video "Why Managing the Hotel Budget Is Like Playing Baseball"

https://qrco.de/bd6gLf

Chapter 44

Understanding the Concept of Owner Spend

The hotel business is unique in that owners, brands and assets all have specific needs that must be addressed. This creates a delicate business balance that must be understood by hospitality financial leaders—people like you and me. Now, this balance isn't terribly complicated. In fact, it hides out in plain sight, so it can be easy to miss if you're not looking for it. Just being on top of the facts will really help. The owner most often wants to talk about the numbers—the *money*—and not the smaller details. So it helps to be ready with the answers.

Owner spend is the key to understanding the relationship between the owner and the brand, and it plays out inside each individual asset on a daily and annual basis in a branded managed hotel. The owner of the asset typically hires a management company—a brand, like Hilton or Fairmont. The brand brings with it the management agreement. The owner pays fees to the brand and is responsible as well for upkeep of the asset and for keeping it in line with brand standards. This is not always clear to the owner at first, and it can become a source of friction.

(When I talk about owner spend, I'm referring to hotels with full-blown management contracts with a brand—not franchised properties, where the concept does not work the same way. But in hotels with full-scale management agreements in place, how that agreement works is the key to the brand's success or failure—and it all revolves around the concept of owner spend.)

Put simply, "owner spend" means the owner spends 100% of what's required to run the hotel. That's right: the owner. Never the brand. This obviously gives the brand the upper hand in dealing with both owner and asset.

The owner writes the checks for everything the hotel needs. Every dollar of operating payroll, executive compensation, capital spend, advertising cost, promotion cost, severance cost, employee benefits and even service-length-of-tenure gifts. I could fill this page and the next one with what the hotel spends its money on. The owner pays every penny of this, never the brand.

What's more, the brand—by way of the Hotel Management Agreement (HMA)—gets to tell the owner exactly what needs to be spent in operating costs on an annual basis. There can be owner pushback on some items, but overall the brand has license through the HMA to get the owner to spend money on anything and everything. Usually the spend is dictated in support of maintaining the standard for the brand. And this "standard" can be nebulous and constantly evolving in areas like training, service, technology, administration . . . you name it. The brand creates it, charges the owner for it—and the owner pays.

Having high brand standards is an excellent way to grow a brand, but it comes with some hurdles. It can be a real problem for owners when assets are not performing. Brands face incredible pressure from owners in times of economic turmoil. Owners want brands to trim the sails and throw as much off the sinking ship as possible. Most brands help in such circumstances by way of Cost Containment Plans (CCP) when occupancy and rates plummet. These help reduce payroll and expenses—for example, authorizing two towels instead of three, closing the concierge service on weekdays, and so on. Before the COVID pandemic we last needed CCPs during the recession of 2008.

But when they are needed, most brands will get into action.

Nonetheless, it's important to point out that even when a hotel faces an economic disaster, regardless of the cause, the owner still pays 100% of the freight. Fees for brand are a percentage of revenue, so even if a hotel's revenue goes down, the owner still has to pay the fees—they don't go away just because profits do.

All this is important to know because if you're a manager or other executive, then you have to deal with the disgruntled owner around things like fees. This is simply the reality of the situation, and like many situations, when the going is good, everyone is happy—but in times of economic challenge the owner/brand relationship can become more adversarial. Lots of times owners will expect the numbers people to create miracles on their behalf because they're hurting. So it's good to know the lay of the land, and to be familiar with the HMA in order to support the hotel.

And you may ask, what's in it for the owner? When all is said and done, after the owner covers all required costs, the owner keeps the profits.

Chapter 45

Understanding the Importance and Use of the Reserve for Capital Replacement

A Hotel Management Agreement (HMA) is like a prenuptial agreement. It defines the relationship between the owner of a hotel and the company that manages it. An HMA delineates who will pay for modifications to the hotel, how disagreements will be arbitrated and a variety of other factors, including the one we'll be talking about in this chapter: the use of the reserve for capital replacement.

The Reserve Account

The reserve account contains money that has been set aside from other active accounts in order to be used for specific needs at a later date. These needs might include modifications to the hotel, capital improvements and other expenses.

It is essential that hotel operators ensure the reserve is properly funded per the terms of the HMA. The reserve serves as an important tool for protecting the operator's rights and the long-term viability of the hotel. Many people mistakenly think the reserve account is the owner's responsibility and that it's therefore up to the owner to determine and ultimately control the funding.

Nope. The manager has both a right and a duty to ensure the proper use of the reserve account using the clauses that are in the HMA.

It's important to become familiar with the reserve and how its use impacts the ultimate success of the hotel. This includes the hotel's value as well as the value of the management agreement. One could say that there's something for everyone here!

First and foremost, the intended use of the reserve account is to ensure the hotel is kept looking and functioning at a high standard. It's essential that both owner and brand ensure and support this objective. If it were left to the owner to decide how much to fund a reserve, it could easily end up that when the hotel is in need of maintenance the money is not there. For example, let's say an owner could decide to fund the reserve and only does it when the hotel is doing well financially. So, during fat periods the reserve is fat, and during lean periods it's lean. But what if improvements during the lean period would help draw in more revenue? It's quite possible that the money wouldn't be there. The owner may have decided to use the money for other needs and the operator will be left high and dry. So, in most cases the reserve should be funded whether or not the hotel is making its profit targets.

Owners are often quick to request (or demand!) that reserving be stopped when the hotel faces a bad year or a cash crunch. This is because reserving money takes it out of the owner's pockets. Operators need to be on their toes and hold the owner's feet to the fire to do what is necessary. Protecting the operator's rights is what is at stake here. Although it may appear counterintuitive to have the manager insist the owner fund the reserve when facing a cash shortage, this is often what's required. The contentious nature of the situation is why it's written into the HMA in the first place, so that it's not a matter for debate. The reserve is essential for the ultimate long-term success of the hotel. It's so important because if the property is properly funded, it ensures there is money for renovations to keep the hotel looking great—and this is in the best interests of the owner and the management company, which is ultimately what everyone wants.

The clause or clauses in your HMA will outline the amount to be set aside in the reserve account. In some cases, the cash must also be transferred into a special bank account to ensure its availability and separation from operating funds. Look closely at the exact wording in the HMA paragraphs covering use of the reserve account. Look for words like "funding" and "transfers." Normally the amount in question for reserving is somewhere between three and five percent of total monthly revenue. However, it is common for a new hotel to have a period where less or even no funding is necessary until the end of the capital funding grace period.

The REVPAR Test

As noted, the reserve funds future improvement and keeps a property competitive. This helps to ensure the hotel's longevity, an important aspect for the operating company, as it helps to protect the all-important management fees. If the hotel fails to stay ahead of its competition and loses its market share, the hotel management company can also lose the right to manage the hotel. The REVPAR test is sometimes included in HMAs for the purpose of protecting the owner should the management company not perform adequately. So, it is imperative that the manager ensure the reserve is properly funded and spent to keep the hotel "fresh" and to maintain at least adequate performance.

The Annual Profit Target Test

The other test that is constantly being evaluated is the annual profit target test. Most HMAs will have a clause that defines the profit test. When it comes to the hotel's performance, everything is tied together. Customers want fresh, up-to-date hotels, and the hotel needs a constant supply of business. A hotel's competition will obviously be making steady improvements. And of course a hotel's profits go up and down based on its performance in the market. So the proper use of the capital reserve is inextricably linked to the ongoing success of the hotel and whether it meets its annual profit targets (independent of the REVPAR index). Most HMAs will state something along the lines of: if the asset does not meet its profit target two years in a row, the owner is free to dismiss the hotel operator. So if operators allow improper use of the reserve they are shooting themselves in the foot!

Be vigilant when it comes to protecting the rights of the operator and know that owners will sometimes try and distract you from your prize—a solid, well-funded reserve that leads to a well-managed and well-capitalized hotel.

Watch a short video on the "Reserve for Capital Replacement"

https://qrco.de/bd6g45

VI

EFFECTIVE LEADERSHIP WITH THE NUMBERS

Managing the numbers in the hotel can be tricky business. Money and numbers have power in our culture, and therefore you need to conduct yourself accordingly. Learning how to lead your team with the numbers isn't hard—it just takes the right approach.

Chapter 46

The General Manager's Yardstick

G enerally speaking, the typical General Manager—at least the ones I have seen, worked with, and gotten to know over the last three-and-a-half decades—is hard-working, dedicated and a bit of an egomaniac.

Let's face it: to rise to the top in any vocation you need to have all three of these traits. They are not handing out keys to the Oval Office to the meek and mild or the stay-at-home crowd. The job of a GM is incredibly demanding, and its responsibilities are huge. The hotel never closes, the guests always want something, and employees are never satisfied. There is always a pot of trouble cooking, and it is usually spiced with all sorts of mystique and intrigue.

GMs usually come from the sales world or have an operations background—which makes complete sense given the long hours and schmoozing required for the job. They need to bring energy, enthusiasm, creativity, and passion to their work.

What the typical GMs do not bring to their role are, unfortunately: administrative skills, focus, computer skills, finance knowledge, business acumen, and—most importantly—any interest in learning these skills.

GMs rely in large part on their financial person to carry the day. And why not? The hotel is full of parallel examples: reliance on the Chef to hold the expertise of the kitchen, produce great food and not poison anyone in the process. Reliance on the Director of

Maintenance to make sure the boilers and chillers are operating. Reliance on the Human Resources Manager to ensure personnel rules are followed and the appropriate benefits programs are in place. You would never expect to see the GM jump into the middle of any of these functions because that is not their job. They correctly rely on the expertise of these professionals to keep the train on the tracks.

If something goes amiss in any of these areas, the owner or brand are typically sympathetic and either grant a pass or add resources to fix the problem.

What the GMs do not and should not get a pass on is poor financial management. After all, finances are a pillar of the hotel business, right alongside guest services and colleague engagement. All three are front and center in a GM's job description (and their performance is directly related to any financial bonus the GM receives). Guest service scores, employee engagement survey results, and the profits—the 1-2-3 of the hotel business.

So, why don't more GMs jump into the middle of the financial machine and make the kind of splash they typically do with service and engagement? I believe the answer is one we've touched on throughout this book: they do not have the training and experience with the numbers, so they hesitate to challenge the financial person or processes. There are many things going on in the financial world, and they all seem complicated. And who wants to go there anyway? It's accounting and numbers and mumbo-jumbo, balance sheets and technical stuff. So most GMs just tune it all out. Sure, they get and read the P&L—they know what the score is after the match. But few will jump into the ring and wrestle their department heads to the ground in order to create the kind of business that holds these heads responsible for their results. GMs seldom go there because they are unsure of what they do not know.

The typical scenario when dealing with the trifecta of a department head, GM and controller goes something like this: the statements come out and the GM sees that expense spending and labor are out of control—they're over-budget, they didn't make their forecast, and they're spending more than last year, like drunken sailors. And why? The GM asks the controller for an explanation and they convincingly blame the department head who did not do their forecast, and who had little to do with the annual budget because they just do not care. The GM now has another conversation with the department head—and they put the blame squarely on the controller/accountant and his staff, who are certainly inept, because half the stuff in their accounts is old and incorrect. They may claim to have no idea where all the expenses came from.

In other words, there is poor or no communication between the controller and the department head around the numbers.

So what is the GM to do?

He/she has two very different stories. Whom should they believe? The fact is, it's their responsibility for the financial leadership role here. It's their job to reign everybody in and get them on the same page.

It seems every department is in the same boat. No one knows what's going on financially. They are seemingly flying by the seat of their pants. Good months only mean a bad one is around the next corner. Surprises are everywhere—like mines in a field, they just go off when they're least expected. So instead of assuming the leadership role, all too often this mess convinces the GM he should just stay away from the numbers and focus instead on relationships with his direct reports and on trying to get everyone to play well together. The GM often has no idea where to begin to get the hotel's finances in order. He did not sign up for this part of the game. And no one is telling him how to fix it.

Meanwhile, the Asset Manager, Owner and everyone else involved, including the department heads and the Controller, are waiting for leadership and someone to make sense of it all. The GM tries, but usually the effort falls far short of effectiveness because he thinks all the numbers are different—and that there's a magical solution to all the infighting and confusion around who is accountable. He believes the solution lies outside of his scope.

Can't someone just fix this mess?

The Hero of this Story

I met our hero rather early in my career when I was an assistant controller in a five-hundred-room, full-service hotel. I had been on the job for less than a year and my boss announced that he was taking the month of August off and that I would be responsible for putting together the first full draft of next year's budget. This meant several things, but out of all of them my biggest fear was having to talk to our GM. Prior to this my exposure to him was very limited, and he had a reputation for being a tough cookie, to say the least.

As the month went by I set about preparing the budget, until at one point the GM called me to his office. He outlined to me how each manager would present their expenses and payroll and how he would be approving any and all budget submissions before I did anything with their numbers.

Interesting, and somewhat surprising.

But, then again, who was I to say otherwise? I was a super-green rookie.

One by one the managers had their appointments with the GM, and I rode shotgun. He had instructed me to send each one their part of the four-year statement, wherein you could see the annual total for each line of expense and payroll. He then instructed his managers to prepare their expenses for the budget and to have a list of items for each account. No approval would be given on a cost-per-room-occupied or cost-per-cover or percentage-of-revenue basis. He insisted on getting the details, and he made each one of his managers responsible for getting their facts together. I have never seen so many people in accounts payable sifting through files and invoices. The same for payroll. He set the standard.

Each manager needed:

- An approved staffing guide for the budget
- A finalized list of salaried positions for the fixed payroll
- A formula for each employee in variable/scheduled (as opposed to salaried) positions that was equal to or better productivity than what was in the previous four-year report.

The meetings were telling. Several managers were shown the door and told the information they had was either incomplete or that it had "too many dollars." The GM simply looked at the information and asked what was in the expense line, comparing the four-year summary for each line, and the departmental total. The same was done with payroll and line-by-line productivity. Not rocket science, but he sure had his managers in line. Several managers made return visits to present their numbers again until they got it right and had his approval. The material that was given to me for the budget model was already approved.

I quickly changed my feelings about this man from distrust and fear to respect and admiration. This guy knew how to manage his team. He was fair and objective, and if you had good reasons for increases he listened and—more than anything else—asked good questions. I just sat there and took it all in—a great lesson on management, organization, and budgeting. I will never forget what he taught me that August. In that month I learned more about the inner workings of each department in the hotel than I had in the previous five years. That is what a good budget process will teach you.

Many of his managers came to see me after their meetings to whine about their budget ordeal with the GM. I would listen and commiserate. But here's one very important thing to note: after they all passed muster with the boss, the level of their knowledge and engagement around their numbers went through the roof. They had to know what was in their accounts and payroll, and the boss used budget season to get them all into shape. From this exercise he took the review process to another level. Every month in the following year he would do the same one-on-one review of their departmental monthly financial results.

This guy was on top of his business.

Back to Budget Season

When my boss returned I was somewhat sad that he did. I was having a lot of fun with the budget and the GM. Two weeks later, it was time to go to a nearby city to present the budget to the corporate team, including the company's CEO and a long cast of other characters. This would be the GM and my boss doing the presenting; it was, as we like to call it, the dog and pony show. To my complete surprise, my boss came into my office a couple of days before the scheduled review with corporate and said, "The GM wants you to go with him to present. You did the work, and he wants you there with him."

Wow! Was I in shock.

Two days later I was on a helicopter with the GM on our way to the presentation. Here I was, the rookie Assistant Controller, helping to present my hotel's budget to the corporate people. Although my GM did most of the talking (I don't remember saying much), he did take a moment when we were done and the budget was approved to tell the corporate squad what a great job I had done putting the budget together in the absence of my boss (the Controller). It was a great moment for me and my young career.

I can honestly say that I have not worked with a GM since who had as much interest or backbone when it came to the numbers. GMs often leave it up to the Controller to try and sort out the actual needs and the BS from department managers. This causes a lot of wasted time and effort. Usually, the managers have rose-colored glasses when it comes to budgeting. They think budget time is when they can right all the wrongs (overspending) from the previous periods by adding copious amounts of payroll and expenses to the budget. This then gets flushed out with budget consolidations and reviews, but what happens, as a result, is that people waste an inordinate amount of time and typically get discouraged and feel put upon, because they do not get what they want in their budgets. All of this is nonproductive work.

In the many years since then that I've prepared budgets, in my opinion the only GM who got the entire process right was the one in the story I just shared. He took the time to organize his department heads, and he used the budget process to educate them, himself and me on what was going down in each area of his hotel. That is how it should be, and it's an approach I've encouraged ever since. It's not magic—but the results are magical.

I vividly remember a boss once telling me that the budget is the GM's yardstick. It is his responsibility to get his managers to come to the table with what they need to run their departments. It is also his responsibility to make sure they understand what they have for payroll and expenses to operate their department. Equally important is what

they do not have to play with.

Most GMs do not use their yardstick. Why? They think the financial piece is some weird concoction of computers and numbers, all things outside of their purview and responsibility. But that's not the case. Numbers are just as important as the other pillars that support the hotel. The GM just needs to take an interest—and control—and more likely than not they'll ultimately gain facility and greater comfort with how the numbers play out in the business.

The Moral of the Story

That GM did not know squat about accounting. He did not know the difference between a debit or a credit. All he needed to do his job and become a stalwart support of his hotel was a keen interest in knowing that his department heads had their financial act together.

Chapter 47

FTARW: The Secret Recipe to Create Financial Leadership in Your Hotel

To get your non-financial managers to play ball with their numbers in your hotel you need a system that they can follow, a sort of roadmap they can use to stay on track every month. Teach them this and you will have an engaged team that buys into playing their financial part.

FTARW is a step-by-step process you can teach your leaders to follow. I have clients who use a whiteboard or a scoring sheet and they display the monthly results. How? They list the leaders who have P&L responsibility down the left-hand side of the sheet and across the top they have five columns; Forecast, Track, Adjust, Review and Write. One client even calls it the "wall of fame." They populate the sheet with X's where the corresponding leaders have completed their part of the recipe for financial leadership that month. What they find is leaders want to have a full set of check marks. Competition is healthy, and so is accountability in a fun and inclusive setting.

"F" stands for Forecast. Did you complete and submit your forecast this month? Was the forecast used? In other words, was it in line with the business volumes relative to the budget? Did the corresponding leader complete the zero-based expenses forecast for their area of responsibility? Zero-based is a list of items and amounts to spend for these items that correspond to each general ledger account they own. The expense forecasting is a mental hurdle that is only overcome by doing the work. The first time is always the hardest. After that, it gets much, much easier. Start with the latest value you have for each account. Maybe it's the budget, maybe it's last month's total, or the same month last year. Grab the GL details for the same account and see what you spent. Knowing your department, what will you need to spend next month? What projects or changes in business standards will drive your activities next month? Make your grocery shopping list for each GL expense account you own. Summarize these account totals and compare that to the total expense values in the budget. Is the forecasted amount reasonable given the forecasted business volumes? If the occupancy is budgeted at 75% and the latest forecast says 77% your expenses should be in line. If the latest forecast is down to say 65%, your expenses need to be reduced. What items from your grocery list can you reduce, postpone or eliminate? And remember the golden rule when it comes to budgets and forecasts, the only thing we know for sure is the number we have is wrong. You will never get it 100% right, ever. So, give it up and put down what you think you will spend relative to your budget and business volumes. Make your list. Forecasting payroll in your department depends on a fixed vs. variable formula. If you're a non-operating department the best way to forecast payroll is to have a monthly schedule with rates of pay multiplied by the wage rates for each position. Consider holidays and vacation days by person/position and you have the forecasted payroll expense. Compare this to the budget and the business volumes forecasted and if your payroll is too high, who can you send on vacation? Whose hours need to be reduced? What can you do to manage the outcome? And remember, you're the manager of the department and that is part of the deal. For variable payroll, you need to have a simple formula that drives the monthly schedule. Let's say you're forecasting the front desk. Both daytime shifts have one person as fixed, and you know that for every 75 arrivals and departures you need an additional eight hours.

Set up your monthly schedule with the daily occupancy, arrivals, and departures for the rooms forecast and you now have the variable hours.

Forecasting revenues: If your department generates revenue, then you need to forecast it day by day. I'll use the spa as an example. To forecast my revenues, I need to set up a 31-day spreadsheet. Down the left, I list all my services in one column, and I put prices in the next column. Each day I indicate how many of my services are purchased. Across the top, I have occupancy by transient and group. I also include other information that is pertinent to my business—like members, social events, weddings—whatever drives my spa. Very quickly I can see the daily sales and the monthly total. Does it make sense based on the business volumes for the hotel? Is there a good chance I can make it? And don't forget the golden rule. You will never be right. If you run an F&B outlet you will need the same basic set up, but more along the lines of meal periods, covers, average cover and rooms capture. If you're forecasting banquets it's day by day, group by group. What do the contracts say? How about the latest intelligence from the conference services people and the catering managers? The information you need for all your forecasting is easily within your grasp. What you need to do is own it, and if pieces are missing you need to pull them together. No one will do this for you.

"T" stands for Track. Tracking the results every day in my hotel is paramount to my department's success. Tracking the revenues every day and month to date along with tracking my spending is the way you do it. Are we on track to make our revenues? Back to the spa example from above, I need to track my treatments relative to my day-by-day estimates. How am I doing? This tracking is how my forecasting gets better and better. Are the expenses I forecasted tracked? Do I know how much I have spent? Do I know how much of my forecasted payroll is scheduled? Tracking the revenue and my spend is how we know what to manage. Tracking back to my monthly expense list via a checkbook and payroll plan is the only way to know what the score is. A cautionary note here: Don't rely on accounting or some system to tell you. You need to know what you have to use and how much you have used relative to the revenues.

"**A**" stands for Adjust. Why do we zero-base our expenses and payroll? Because we want to be able to adjust our spend as business volumes change. It's called managing—managing what my department consumes relative to the business volumes and revenues. This is where the magic happens with our formula. If I don't keep a close eye on revenues and don't know how much I can spend on each item and how many hours of payroll I can use, then I'm lost. I want to be able to manage my costs relative to revenues. If business levels are on target, then I know I can spend what I planned. If business levels are below forecast I know I need to do my part and spend less. From my detailed lists of payroll and expenses, what do I need to adjust? I need to make these adjustments. No one will do this for me. I own it and I own the result for my department.

"**R**" stands for Review. I have put a reasonable amount of effort into creating the forecast for my area and I have tracked my expenses and my payroll hours. Now it's showtime. All this activity will be reported in the financials. The P&L and the general ledger listing hold the results. I want to closely review these instruments to make sure that what gets reported is what happened. I want to know what I bought and how much should be reflected in the account details. I want to make sure the activity in the account and the value in the P&L mirror my information. This step can be frustrating and your partner on the financial side must be willing to take responsibility for any mistaken postings, old items, corporate charges, and so on. With this partnership, these surprises will diminish. Without your vigilant review, your other work is meaningless. Own this. You want to see the results of your efforts pointing to numbers that you made happen. Work with the accounting team to ensure they get it right. Repeat this every month and you will get your accounts clean.

"W" stands for Write. Every hotel has some form of monthly commentary to the owners, brand or management team. Its contents disclose what happened. It tells the story the financials cannot tell by themselves. You write your part of the story. What happened in your department with your accounts? What assumptions were right and which ones were wrong, and why? What was over and what was under, and why? You don't regurgitate numbers—you tell your story, whatever it is. Our business is not a science and you will never get it 100%, ever. So, stop craving perfection and start wrapping your arms around your piece of the pie.

Then get ready. It's time to start over again.

Remember this. The money, aka forecast, budget, P&L, is one of the three pillars. The job will never be completely mastered. We just start over and work the system every month to get better. That's the hotel business.

Watch a short video on the "System to Use in Your Hotel to Create Financial Leadership"

https://qrco.de/bd7FJc

Chapter 48

Is Your Hotel Culture Based on Blame or Appreciation?

B lame and appreciation.
   In my career, I have seen both. Lots of appreciation for hard work in a challenging workplace, and—on the flipside—horror stories about blame for mistakes made and lack of preparedness.

Blame

Blame is the easy one to "master." I like to refer to the technique as "management by embarrassment." One of my previous hotels was a classic blame-game hotel. After a much-publicized error, screw up or service interruption, the GM would warmly say, "Where is my victim?" or, "Bring me the victim." What usually followed was tantamount to a public flogging.

Everyone got their turn. Everyone got used to watching in stunned disbelief—thankful it wasn't their turn that day—while the victim took their "punishment."

The weekly department head meeting was both somewhat entertaining and horrific at the same time. Each week someone would be singled out. There was always at least one victim, but sometimes several people would experience the wrath of our GM—quite often for the simplest, seemingly meaningless things. No one escaped without a turn in the hot seat. Many times, there were tears, and many people cited such moments as why they moved on to new jobs.

In one instance a sales manager was asked about the pickup report from the previous day. She had the numbers right, and it had been a slow day.

Our GM asked her, "Do you know how to sell?"

She answered, "Yes . . ." with hesitation in her voice.

She knew it was her turn.

The oxygen was sucked from the room as we collectively gasped and looked around the table at one another in horror.

She was innocent—her only crime was being in sales. Nonetheless, it was her turn to take it on the chin.

"Sell me this pencil," he said to her.

She tried to respond, but her words were garbled at best.

He continued, "Find out what kind of pencil I want, you moron! Then tell me why your pencil is exactly the one I need."

She was quickly reduced to tears, and in the ensuing silence she left the room. With the carnage complete the agenda continued.

I had a meeting with the GM immediately afterwards, and I asked him, "Why do you pick on people, singling them out and embarrassing them in front of their peers?"

He smiled and said, "I'm an actor doing my job. And it's my job to hold these people accountable and maintain control."

I told him there are other ways to do that. He said he knew that, but they weren't as much fun.

Old habits die hard. A month later our executive team (about ten of us) went on a retreat. The facilitator did an exercise where we went around the table focusing on one person at a time; everyone else would say what we liked and did not like about the way we worked with that person.

Our GM was last. I was first in the rotation to tell him what I liked and did not like. I told him I really appreciated his passion and creativity. Then came the hard part: "We spoke about this before, one-on-one," I told him. "Your habit of singling a person out at the weekly meeting is shameful, and in my opinion it's the biggest problem that could be easily solved—just stop doing it."

You could have heard a pin drop.

He simply nodded his head, and my turn was over. Well, one after another, the next nine executives told him the exact same thing, "Stop being such a bully."

I learned two big lessons from this experience: bullies are not only found on the playground, and people can change. After that retreat, the GM changed his approach, and the weekly meetings lost their victim-blaming aspect and became far more productive.

Appreciation

It should be obvious how much of a difference it can make when people feel appreciated. This is something there's not enough of in the work-world. When things go well we tend to simply feel relieved—or we hold our breath in anticipation of things going wrong! The flipside is simply acknowledging when things go right— and sharing appreciation for the people who are part of that process. Things can go wrong, sure—but you can still be appreciative of people's efforts and commit to being fair and reasonable as you move forward. "Create" and "nurture" can be the buzzwords here. Approach people with the assumption that they want things to work out as much as you do. Offer praise and recognition when appropriate. Doing so doesn't mean you're a "softie" or a pushover. It means you recognize the importance of every individual in your operation. People will feel this attitude in you—whether they're colleagues, superiors or subordinates—and most likely it will spark a mutual feeling of appreciation in them.

Now more than ever in hospitality we need to create a safe and attractive place for our colleagues to call home.

Chapter 49

The Morning Meeting

The morning meeting is a mainstay in almost every hotel. All the key department managers and leaders gather for it, usually in the front office or sometimes in an in-house meeting room, to devour the day's business. It's a great way to distribute last-minute information and highlight important changes to groups and business volumes. You may not be invited to these meetings—yet!—if you're not a manager, but knowing what takes place in them will help prepare you as you progress in the hotel business, and also give you greater insight into daily operations in the hospitality world.

If you're a manager, the morning meeting is a key part of your day. It's your moment to shine. Come with an agenda and assume a leadership role. It's a chance to create a team environment in which everyone contributes something of value and everyone leaves with something of value.

A hotel is a big, busy place, and you can go months without seeing or talking to people unless you create the time to do it. So the morning meetings are where Housekeeping can find out what's going on in Maintenance as it impacts their rooms, the restaurant can connect with Guest Services about exciting offerings, Accounting can learn what Sales and Marketing efforts are underway, and so on. This is valuable stuff that leads to better results and better service.

Despite this, you'll soon realize that not everyone wants to attend. But this is another important aspect of personal growth in the hotel business, whether you're the GM or someone on the way up: this is where you can start to build a deeper understanding of the inner workings of the hotel.

All this said, many morning meetings miss the most important pieces of information. So let's go through a rundown of what's usually talked about, and what's left off the table. First, here's a typical agenda:

- Previous day's occupancy, rate and REVPAR.
- Anticipated occupancy, rate and REVPAR for that night.
- VIP arrivals and departures.
- Previous day's security and safety report.
- Restaurant summary: yesterday and today, covers, issues.
- Housekeeping sick calls for today, rooms out of order.
- Banquet activity yesterday and today, special needs.
- Maintenance report, noting special activity, getting rooms back.
- Guest complaints and compliments received, follow-up.
- Rooms pickup report for the previous day.
- Labor summary with variances to plan.
- Human resources update, with a highlight on training.

All of this is usually good, pertinent information—vital facts that department heads need in order to get on with their day. So what's missing?

What's missing is a review of the business strategy and how the execution of that strategy is unfolding.

What's missing is the big-picture information about what each department head needs to do today, tomorrow and next week in order to right the ship or keep it sailing in the proper direction. Each manager in the meeting holds their piece of the business, and they need to know whether the vessel is on track to make its forecast revenues or not and—most importantly—what they need to do so their part of the enterprise flows.

The 1.2.3. Strategy

A 1.2.3. strategy for managing the finances needs to be clearly understood and acted upon by each member of the team who manages a work schedule or orders their department's supplies.

What exactly are the monthly forecast business volumes, rooms revenue, food and beverage revenue, other revenues? What is my department payroll productivity target for the month? What are the detailed zero-based expenses for my department? It's not too much to expect that each one of your key managers knows these facts, because this information is just as important as guest service execution and colleague engagement. Expectation is the wrong word here. That is, at this point everyone will have agreed to know and manage these business facts. The key part of the execution of the leaders is knowing their numbers: They put the numbers together for their area.

Step 1 is developing a management team that knows the business strategy and plays the "business of hotels" daily. Everyone must know the latest score. Where exactly are we with our business volumes? It's like the last month of the baseball season. Is your team going to make it into the playoffs? That's the level of focus you need here. This is tricky, and it requires insight, experience, and a steady hand.

And so, **Step 2** is that every day your leadership needs to get the latest pickup on rooms, conference services, outlets and other sales. Where are we, and what is the prediction for the month-end result? Waiting for the fifteenth of the month to take our pulse and see how things look on the revenue front is a dangerous practice. You need to be on top of the revenue picture from day one—and every day after that. Nothing is more important to your business success than having your managers understand the latest projected revenues by department for the entire month at hand.

Step 3 is deciding what to do when the ship needs to turn. This is where 90% of hotels are completely lost. If occupancy is soft and my room revenue is going to be short compared to my budget, what moves do my teammates make to manage the flow thru? If my rate is down to forecast, what expenses can be managed so I can positively affect the costs this month? If my banquet or restaurant volumes are not going to come together as planned, I need my managers to do their part. This is where we go back to steps 1 and 2. If I have trained my managers well and we have done a good job with our "distant early warning" system to help them understand the revenue picture, then I have a chance. If my managers know their staffing guidelines and follow them to the letter—daily—they will still have a good shot at making the productivity target for their individual area. If I have a team of leaders who all know what is in their expense lines—in detail—then they will know when to adjust spend and how to turn the ship.

It is not rocket science. It is just attention to the details and making sure all my sailors do their parts. As the GM or the Director of Finance, I cannot turn the ship when there are late calls for a man overboard. My crew needs to know their part of the ship inside out, and they need to know how the wind is blowing. If a storm is coming, they need to do their part. If the seas are calm and it is smooth sailing, they need to keep doing what they're doing.

Your morning meeting is your daily view into the latest forecast for the month, and it's the place where you create the plays that will help you win the game. Throwing your hands up in the air and believing there is nothing we can do when a problem arises late in the game is just poor management.

Execute the 1.2.3. strategy in your hotel and watch the collective abilities of your management team grow.

Watch this short video on the "Morning Meeting"

https://qrco.de/bd6Yhb

Chapter 50

The Forecast Disconnect and How to Correct It

When I work with hotel clients around their financial leadership it's often centered on getting the team to do their monthly financial forecast. A greater interest in doing it produces better and more consistent results. When doing financial leadership workshops and individual coaching, I inevitably discover the same thing time and time again: a disconnect between the Executive Team/Director of Finance part of the operation and the department line managers.

In this chapter, I am going to explain why this disconnect exists, how to detect it and what you can do to fix it.

Why the Disconnect?

The disconnect exists for two main reasons.

One, we all come from a world where the numbers have forever been in the closet. We now want them to come out and we don't know how to get that to happen. We don't naturally know how to make them part of the mainstream communication inside our hotel. I teach my clients to make the numbers just as accessible as guest service information and colleague engagement content.

Two, we almost always create the forecast to satisfy the masters, the brand and the owner. We construct this forecast on tight timelines, and that usually means it's whipped up by the financial leader with some inputs from the executive only. We do not take the time to get the line department managers involved in the creation of the monthly financial forecast. This is a big turnoff for anyone who then must have anything to do with that forecast. No input from me equals zero buy-in and accountability.

How to Detect the Disconnect?

I often do an exercise in my workshops where I ask the participants to pair up and work together. Their assignment is to come up with just one word that describes the current financial leadership culture in their hotel. After they choose their word, they need to come back to the group and tell us what it is and why they chose that word. This is where the disconnect is easily seen. Words like: *secret, isolated, elitist, club,* and *puzzled* are very common, and this points directly to the diagnosis. When I ask each presenter to explain why they chose their word, the reason is usually that they don't participate in the forecast or, if they do, they have no idea how the final numbers come together.

Bingo! We have just exposed the problem. Sometimes this is all it takes to start the cure. If the GM is in the room and people are brave enough to speak (if the culture is open enough) we can have a productive discussion on why this condition exists and how to fix it. Short of doing the exercise yourself, just ask some of your line managers if their numbers are in this month's forecast. You will know pretty quickly what the answer is.

What Can You Do to Remedy the Disconnect?

Line managers want to take responsibility for their numbers. They want to be the ones who create these numbers and own them so long as it's safe and productive to do so. The following conditions need to exist in order to foster open communication around the forecasted numbers and how the hotel is performing relative to that forecast.

We need to clearly identify and make agreements with the line managers around who is responsible for each line of revenue, cost of goods, payroll and expense in our profit and loss statement. Ensuring someone owns each line is the first critical step and one that we cannot overlook. Simply assigning the rooms accounts to the room's division manager is not going to cut it. We need to step sideways to the front office manager, the housekeeper, the guest services manager and the reservations manager and clearly agree on who owns each account. Many expense lines have multiple uses, so having one owner who can corral the others is critical. Knowing who owns each line also allows us to more clearly see the operation and who is and who's not on top of their numbers.

We want to make sure that each member of our management team prepares their own forecast and we want to make sure that we use their forecast. This means that they are plugged into the schedule and that they allow themselves the time to do their part of the forecast. In turn, this also means the Director of Finance provides clear communication on the schedule and allows time to do the consolidation—and most importantly gets back to each line manager when changes are necessary to meet the overriding goals of the forecast. If we ask for the forecast from the line managers and then change it, or don't use it, we have just spoiled the entire process. This is where most hotels fall off the rails. They may ask for the forecast and get it, but it is either changed or not used, and this is the poison pill that creates the disconnect.

Now that we have the line managers' forecast inside our final monthly financial forecast, we're off to the races. The next step is making sure that each day we talk about the room's pick-up and the banquet/catering pace, as well as the restaurant and bar volumes at our morning meeting.

Are we going to make our numbers? This is the question we want each line manager to be obsessed with. If we're not going to make our revenues, we need our line managers to adjust accordingly. This is the pivot, and it's what we train for. Adjusting the schedule and the purchase orders to reflect the change in business volumes is what we want our line managers to do. This allows us the opportunity to manage our flow thru. Without the line managers preparing and using their own forecasts, we're like a ship in a storm without a rudder.

Conclusion

There you have it. If you have a forecast disconnect in your hotel you now know the probable cause and the cure. Having the leadership team plugged into the real forecast and managing the middle of your statement is priceless. It's also a lot more fun for everyone.

Chapter 51

The Three Dimensions of Delegation

"I don't have a problem with delegation. I love to delegate. I am either lazy enough, or busy enough, or trusting enough, or congenial enough, that the notion of leaving tasks in someone else's lap doesn't just sound wise to me, it sounds attractive."

~ John Ortberg

The art of delegation is often misunderstood. In this chapter we'll look at how to use the three powerful dimensions of delegation to be more productive, develop our own abilities and help others become more accomplished as well.

First off, let's examine what delegation is all about and clear up some misunderstandings.

I was not a fan of being delegated to early in my career. I thought I was being "put upon" when someone delegated their work to me. I vividly remember a day when my boss at the time came into my office to give me yet another assignment, one that had previously been his task. I'd been in what was for me the new and challenging role of Assistant Controller for about six months, and most days I was drowning in work.

Yet here he was again, giving me a report to put together to send to corporate by Tuesday.

This was the straw that broke the camel's back.

"Why do I have to do another one of your chores?" I asked,

244 ← EFFECTIVE LEADERSHIP WITH THE NUMBERS

frustrated.

"Listen, David," he said. "I get to decide who is ready for more assignments around here, and if you're half as smart as I think you are, you will do the same!"

Wow, that hit me like a ton of bricks. My initial reaction was: What a conceited and shallow attempt to manipulate me while dumping his work on my plate.

This, I believed, was his MO, and, to add insult to injury, he was even doggedly proud of it. It hit me hard. There was no way I was going to be able to swim with this stuff piling up and a never-ending supply of new bunk to deal with.

I worked late that evening and on my walk home I was replaying the episode with my boss when I had an epiphany.

"If you are half as smart as I think you are, you will do the same."

What exactly did that mean? How was I going to do the same? What was the real message inside that envelope? I thought long and hard about this, and the following day I decided to get some clarity. I went to see my boss and asked him to tell me how I should be using delegation in my role as Assistant Controller.

He smiled and said, "I was wondering how long it would take for you to wake up."

Then he explained his view of the hotel finance office work world. It went like this: the work never stops coming. The assignments from corporate, the owners and the GM are not going away. In fact, they are going to get more and more frequent. That's just the way it is. Our job is to ensure these assignments are dealt with properly, and to do this we have to delegate work to others.

I'll never forget what he said about that: "If you know how to do something, it is time to give it up and teach someone else how to do it."

"But how?" I asked. "Everyone is so busy."

"By finding out what people want, and helping them get it," he said.

This sounded like a con if ever there was one.

But he explained further: all people want to grow, to have greater responsibility and to move ahead in their careers and lives.

And that is what we constantly need to be looking for and developing in our teams—an attitude of learning and progression. If we assume people are at their limits or don't want to grow, then we effectively just shut down the machine. Our job—and, quite frankly, everyone's job—is to teach and develop, and the fuel for this growth is the work we do.

Once he explained it to me that way, I began to see what he meant. The big question then became: could I learn to do the same?

The first dimension of delegation: **be a mentor and trusted guide**.

The following day I sat down with our credit manager, who was relativity new and green. I asked her what her goal was in the next two years. She said quite clearly that it was to get out of the credit roll and onto a path to be an accountant and eventually a controller.

I surprised myself by what I did in response. I offered to help her get there by showing her how to do some journals and reconciliations. I told her that it would be an additional workload, but also that I could help her with developing her credit and collections assistant—who was chomping at the bit to become the credit manager.

At that moment it seemed like someone changed the music in our office from a dreary tune to something with a fresh and uplifting beat. These development exercises continued, and it was not long before I could see a much stronger and more meaningful team developing.

I know what some of you are probably thinking: most of your colleagues are maxed out with their work, and on top of that, they don't want to move ahead. They're happy just where they are.

This thinking will get you nowhere fast. It is victim-thinking, and you need to turn it around, own it, and find a way to lead that gives everyone an opportunity for development.

People naturally want to make a difference. They just need to see that it's possible. It's your job to create an environment in which this can happen, and to have those heartfelt conversations that lead to a process of continual creation and reinvention in your staff.

The work we do is the fuel for development. When the work is properly positioned it takes on a whole new light. Think back, if you will, to your own development. Who helped you? Which individuals took you under their wings? I am willing to bet that you would move heaven and earth for them, such is your gratitude. This is the kind of relationship you want to be constantly developing in your teams.

The second dimension of delegation is **your own growth**. Delegation allows you to clear your own path to take on newer and bigger assignments. As you hand off processes and procedures with which you're already familiar to others—supporting them in their growth—you can open yourself up to expanding your own skillset.

The people in your organization will see this and your career will be supercharged, because you will be demonstrating your ability to lead and expand.

The third dimension is **innovation**.

People always surprise me with their abilities to create new and innovative ways to do things. It's human nature that often, once we learn how to do something, we keep doing it the same way forever after. But the moment we delegate a task, an opportunity opens up. A fresh set of eyes and an engaged mind can lead to improvements in familiar procedures and processes.

A great example is the credit manager I mentioned above. She was just a few years younger than me and more than just a little comfortable with the process of creating macros. She automated several of the journals and created a calendar tab process for the reconciliations. Both processes saved considerable time.

This is the by-product of learning and development—new and continuous innovation.

"Delegation is giving others the opportunity to participate in the story. If you have a good story, people will line up to get involved—to play a part in the story." ~ Eric Phillips

Watch a short video: "Learn How to Delegate—It's Magic"

https://qrco.de/bd6gDa

Chapter 52

How a Boring Routine Secretly Equals Power

If you wish you could do more each day and you're open to looking at things differently, open to considering that there may be a stronger system to follow, perhaps this chapter is for you.

When we have a routine, we have a system that helps us generate tremendous results on the core work we do. We cannot be creative outside of a solid routine that gets done everything we need to accomplish on a given day. When the core work is done, we then have a license to create outside of that routine.

Our core responsibilities require a routine to nail them every day, something that allows us to automatically keep up to speed with information, reports, reviews, approvals, signoffs, studies, signatures—whatever you need to absorb and do every day and not fall behind. When we build our routine, we free our minds to really focus on the tasks at hand. We never need to ask ourselves, "What do I need to do this morning?"

Finding and creating your routine is the most powerful tool you have to be an efficient and organized leader. Never falling behind in your work is like never having a losing streak. You win every day by nailing your core work. This creates the time to make the meetings and have the conversations that lead to great ideas, awesome agreements and growth in your leadership. If you're always thinking about the mountain of work you need to get done, you're never really going to have the space to be innovative and the time to build your leadership inside your organization.

Knowing you're on top of your core function is an awesome feeling, like completing a ten-mile run or fifty laps in the pool. It gives you energy, confidence, and a sense of well-being. Imagine . . . all of this from a simple routine. I often hear leaders say how busy and swamped they are with work. Look inside this person's world and you will find they are lacking a solid routine to anchor their lives.

Austin Kleon from his book, *Steal Like an Artist*:

> "The worst thing a day job does is take time away from you, but it makes up for that by giving you a daily routine in which you can schedule a regular time for your creative pursuits. Establishing and keeping a routine can be even more important than having a lot of time. Inertia is the death of creativity. You have to stay in the groove. When you get out of the groove, you start to dread the work, because you know it's going to suck for a while—it's going to suck until you get back into the flow."[6]

This is a powerful switch to turn on—knowing your dedication to your routine is going to pay back, that it's going to give you the time to be creative, to solve big challenges by creating the clean space in your day and in your consciousness. As a leader this is priceless. You didn't sign up to push paper but it's at the core of what you do. By nailing this routine discipline, you now have access to the good stuff. You have in essence paid your dues and now you can get to what you really came here to do: lead and create.

Be boring and crank it out in your routine so you can be brilliant and original in your pursuit of innovation, efficiency and creative leadership. Fail to create a powerful routine and you're forever at the

---

[6] Kleon, Austin. *Steal Like an Artist*. Workman Publishing. 2012.

mercy of being another ineffective leader who is just too busy. Does this sound familiar?

Chapter 53

Let's Bring Multitasking to an End

In the hotel business, we need to be able to differentiate between when it is appropriate to do more than one thing at a time and when it is not.

The simple fact is the human mind can only entertain one thought at a time. If you don't believe me—just try it! Try thinking about two things at once: like what to make for dinner and how you can jazz up the monthly commentary next time around. It's impossible to entertain two thoughts at once. Back and forth works, but never two together at the same time. We're not built that way.

Now, for some of you readers, that's enough to prove my point. For the rest of you, you're going to need more evidence and reasoning—so here we go.

I was once a big fan of doing several things at the same time. Some of my personal favorites were: attending meetings and responding to emails and signing purchase orders, talking on the phone and signing checks, conference calls and signing off on daily operations packages and, my all-time favorite, watching the news channel that constantly played in my boss's office while attending the weekly executive committee meeting. I was convinced that these mundane tasks were all being handled effectively and efficiently by me in a "more than one thing at a time" functional way. It is true that I was able to do all these things and they seemingly got done. However, on closer examination, the output or throughput on all of these was below par.

To understand why we multitask we must consider why we think it's okay, even preferable, to do it in the first place. Most of us in hospitality leadership are *physically* moving around a lot, and it's imperative that we accomplish as many things as possible with each movement or trip. Never take a trip without your hands and tray being full. I vividly remember my captain waiter following me around and telling me what I could and should be adding to each trip in and out of the kitchen/dining room. Early on in this business I was a waiter, and in that role I was all about doing three things at once: a second drink for Mr. Howard, clean napkins for my station and the check for table 12. All of this was accomplished on one trip back to the dining room. At the same time we know we're two minutes out from the entrees being ready for table 9, we see Mrs. Smith heading to the restroom—better get her one of those fresh napkins in the next 90 seconds—table 7 needs clearing and table 10 is ready to order.

Something similar is true for anyone in our industry who has tasks to perform, such as cleaning a room, stocking cupboards, delivering luggage or assembling a meal. All these tasks fall into the category of "automatic"—that is, we can essentially do them without thinking about them. Or at least we can juggle the tasks effectively, like I had to learn to do as a waiter. This positive and essential skill can and should be taught to all service staff to ensure they are productive and work efficiently. It will go a long way in saving time and energy, and in minimizing stress.

The problem is that all too often we carry this ideal from our initial hotel jobs into our roles as supervisors, managers and executives. In this new world of being a manager or executive we need to change gears to function effectively. We are now being paid to think.

That's right, the most important function we perform takes place between our ears. This requires focus and discipline, the ability to concentrate on one thing from start to finish. If you have a short attention span and continually interrupt yourself with competing thoughts and activities, you need to change that behavior now.

How do you know you have a focus problem? Take this simple test: think for two minutes about the most important thing you need to do next. Commence that activity and see how long it takes you to lose focus and think about something else. That focus is a muscle and it needs exercise to remain focused for an extended period. Continue to practice this activity and push yourself to focus longer each time. Your reward will be tasks being complete and done, not half-done and needing to be re-done again and again.

Another telltale sign of the multitasker is that your work rules your day. Do you come to work with 100 things to do and leave twelve hours later with 110? That's because you're trying to do more than one thing at a time and nothing really gets completed. Completed is what you want. Done and never to revisit is your goal!

Chapter 54

Creating Agreements versus Having Expectations

There is a popular saying in America inspired by the slogan for a doughnut and coffee chain: *"America Runs on Dunkin'."* Another thing that our western culture runs on even more than coffee and doughnuts? Expectations. And just like coffee, and especially doughnuts, expectations are really bad for you.

You may be thinking I'm nuts even calling this chapter "Creating Agreements versus Having Expectations." Maybe it sounds kind of Pollyannaish. But I encourage you to read on. I think I can introduce you to a more effective way of managing your relationships in the hotel, and maybe even at home and elsewhere in your personal life. If you can shift in this direction, you're going to be a more effective leader—and people will like you more too. The difference between agreements and expectations may seem subtle, but it's actually huge enough that it can transform your relationships.

I got a lot of the concepts for this chapter from the author of several great books and audio recordings, Steve Chandler. While his take on expectations is not new, his way of explaining the difference between these two ways of operating is nothing short of brilliant.

So why do agreements work better than expectations? First let's think about the difference between them. One way to consider this is that expectations are just that: things that are expected of you. You have no say in the matter. Someone who expects something of you is generally in a position of authority over you. You may feel inferior to them—or at least feel like you're seen as inferior. You may resent expectations and the other person's power over you.

Agreements, on the other hand, are made between two or more parties, and they are obviously agreed upon. Both sides at the table, both sides coming to an agreement about what needs to be done and how to do it. This doesn't mean that no one's the boss. That kind of hierarchy can still exist within the framework of agreements. But it allows input from both sides into the all-important issues of how and when something can get done.

In a nutshell, expectations alienate people; agreements bring them together at the table.

Let's consider this a bit more. Old-school thinking is that if you are the boss, the superior, then your subordinates need to follow your instructions. That's the expectation. But people hate having expectations put on them. On the other hand, agreements can create a strong consensus by opening wide the lines of communication.

By way of illustration, let me share a story about making an agreement, and at the same time seeing the communication for what it was: my wanting someone to do what I needed them to do.

My story takes place around the annual exercise we all love to hate in hospitality: budget season. I used to think that a strong approach meant a tight schedule with dates that gave me time to get everyone's submission, do my consolidation and make changes. But like always, it was a matter of pulling teeth to get the other managers to deliver on my schedule. Why was this so difficult? I gave them lots of time and they knew it was a requirement. Even the stuff I did manage to get on time was of low quality, and I almost always ended up changing it. Why did I bother to chase these people anyway?

Now this particular version of "silly season" was shaping up much like the others—me frustrated and not getting any good budget data—

until something happened quite by accident. It involved our F&B manager. She was relatively new to the position, and after seeing my schedule for budget submissions she asked me for a meeting.

In my experience, this type of meeting usually wound up being a waste of time because I ended up listening to the typical operations person wax on about what they did not know and did not have time to do—namely their budget.

She approached it a bit differently. She asked if I would show her what was needed and where she could find it, to which I replied, "I'll show you if you promise to meet the schedule and do it in detail." To which she responded, "Absolutely. You can count on me."

We met three times on three different days, and I showed her where she could find the numbers she needed for rooms and banquet sales, the detailed items for her expenses and finally the formulas to use for her staffing guide. I was very pleasantly surprised when the same manager asked the following week if we could meet to review her detail before it was submitted. I was even more surprised when I saw what she had put together. It was a very complete and well-thought-out draft of her budget.

It made me think hard about what had just happened over the previous two weeks and, most importantly, why it went down the way it did.

Normally, I send out the schedule, which is all about me and my deadlines. There is no getting away from the fact that, come hell or high water, I need to get the budget done. In the case of the F&B manager, we took a different approach that had the two of us exchanging value with each other.

I isolated four distinct elements of our transaction:

1. We both got something.
2. We both gave something.
3. I showed her where to find things.
4. She committed to the due dates.

So in the end, she got what she wanted—the help she needed—and she gave me the quality information I needed, on time.

The more I thought about this transaction, the more excited I got about what I had discovered. Having coincidentally listened to Mr. Chandler's audio on expectations versus agreements at nearly the same time, I was completely taken aback by how effective this exchange had been.

Finding out how to help someone get what they wanted was the key to getting what I wanted.

Not some one-sided, half-baked "me, me, me" version of an expectation where my needs were the only thing that mattered.

I tried a little experiment the following week and asked another manager point-blank what he needed from me to get his budget done, and done properly. He responded with a smile and half-joked that what he really needed was a new laptop.

So, guess what I did? I flipped the rotation of laptop rollouts so that he got his machine the next day. The funny thing was, I got his submission ahead of time—and he nailed it.

Throughout the entire month leading up to the first budget draft being completed, I did the same "agreement exercise" with several other managers, and **each one delivered**. Obviously this was a win-win, something you can't get with expectations, but which is far more likely when it comes to agreements.

Watch a short video on "Agreements versus Expectations"

https://qrco.de/bd6Yp7

Chapter 55

Inclusivity in Hospitality

I consider myself to be extremely fortunate for many things, but the number one thing is my parents. We were decidedly middle class. My father was an automobile mechanic turned community college instructor and my mom was a homemaker for me, my two brothers and my sister. We were not well off, but we had a home and everything we needed, especially two loving and level-headed parents.

We grew up in a small coastal town in Atlantic Canada. Diversity did not exist. Everyone was Caucasian. I mean everyone. There were no black, brown, or yellow people. The closest thing to diversity of race was a family of First Nations people, perhaps mixed with Korean. But I honestly didn't know they were different. The thing is, I don't remember my parents ever talking about race, one way or the other. It just didn't exist. All I remember about my parents and relating to other people is that you didn't say a bad thing about anyone, period. It was not tolerated. My mother would always say the following about other people who were suffering, or perhaps if we saw a person who was down or who had a problem: "There but for the grace of God go you and I."

I also vividly remember my father telling me that he didn't know anyone. If we wanted to get ahead in life, we would need to work for it. There was no one coming to save us. He also said that we could do or be anything, as long as we were willing to work for it.

From my childhood, I was given a pretty neutral view of the world, probably because of this background: my parents and surroundings, and the fact that we grew up in a fairly remote and sparsely populated place where people were generally kind and helpful.

Fast forward twenty years and I was working in the hotel world. My first two hotels were kind of the same as my hometown, but the third one was a wake-up call. Over a thousand rooms in a big city equals over a thousand employees and the world coming together. There were all kinds of people, different races, languages, dress, food, culture—you name it and it was there.

People in our business know that hotels are pipelines into our communities. For over 140 years, many immigrants in North America have found their way into their first jobs through hotels, in areas like the hotel kitchen, housekeeping, accounting, food & beverage, front office, stewarding—absolutely everywhere.

From this reality comes the fact that in order to be successful in the hotel we need a cohesive team. Departments and people in them need to work together and cross-departmentally as well. No one or no department is an island. No one or no department is better than another.

People work very hard, and long days are the norm in the hotel world. People get put through the wringer, so to speak, and there's a lot of stress. But what keeps people sane is the teamwork and the diversity. This, I believe, is the secret fabric that provides the strength that holds things together. When I'm feeling maxed out, all I have to do is look to the left and right and I see people digging in deeper than I am. I see people who have it worse than me. But there is strength in that, because we all lift each other up—we don't push each other down.

The divisions melt away. You don't see differences of race, ethnicity, gender, sexual orientation, age or anything else, because you're in it together, and just about everyone is in it to win. If you're not, you won't last. To win means get ahead, to prosper, to find your own way. The hotel world is still a place where hope reigns supreme. You can still start in the dish pit and one day be the chief steward, or maître d', or the Sales Manager, or the Controller, or the General Manager or yes, even the company CEO. If your eyes are open, you see this all around you, every day. It's what happens.

Inside the hotel world, there is hope, and all someone needs to do is work for it and they will rise. That's my take on it. I have seen it happen a thousand times.

In life there are two things: love and hate. Everything we do to one another can be stripped down to either one or the other: In the hotel world, love prevails because there is hope and a path forward for everyone as long as you're willing to work for it.

Thanks, Mom and Dad, for showing me this.

Chapter 56

How to Lead in Times of Crisis and Change

The 2023 financial crisis. COVID-19 & the global pandemic. The War in Ukraine. What do all these events have in common? Dramatic and unexpected change that can have a devastating impact on our personal and professional lives. No matter what the crisis du jour, we need to be prepared.

For the hospitality industry, COVID-19 spelled overnight disaster for almost every hotel. Many closed their doors for months. The ones that stayed open during the pandemic furloughed or laid off much of their staff, including managers and supervisors.

The people who were lucky (or unlucky) enough to remain working had three or four—heck, even ten jobs to do. The burnout and lack of satisfaction for those workers was and probably still is severe. New, complicated and expensive protocols for cleaning and service were accompanied by never-ending rules and regulatory changes to customer requirements and access.

For owners, the pandemic lockdowns meant immediate and serious cash-flow problems. Mortgages could not be paid, and in many instances payroll had to be funded from the owners' own pockets. The pandemic meant the largest and longest drop in revenues—the biggest and longest hit to REVPAR—in the history of hospitality.

Yet with all this to overcome, hotels by and large carried on. As I write this several years into COVID, the field is far from leveled. The industry is experiencing some kind of recovery, but we all know things can come off the rails again in an instant. So, what are the lessons learned, and what can we do going forward to ensure recovery is sustainable, not just now with COVID, but whenever a crisis strikes? And how can we ensure the lessons are applied and not forgotten?

In no particular order, here are nine COVID takeaways which will, I think, be relevant in a variety of situations.

Segmentation. Like the old saying goes, "Don't put all of your eggs in the same basket." Having and promoting a diverse market segmentation is so important to your hotel's long-term health. During the pandemic, groups, corporate travel and long-haul leisure were decimated—and they still are. Being able to shift quickly to shorter-term leisure (if you were primarily a group meeting spot), and lots of it, was the key. In a continued recovery, hotels that position and transition themselves best back towards supporting groups, corporate and long-haul leisure will prosper. Hotels need to anticipate changes like these before they happen. Groups have a longer booking window and individual corporate travelers need contracted rates ahead of their resurgence.

Investing In Talent. I think many hotels realize they shot themselves in the foot at the beginning of the pandemic. It may have been a mistake to release so many people ahead of government programs that would have given employers better long-term options to retain employees—and potentially avert the massive labor shortages that often ensued after the pandemic. Our talent takes time to cultivate, and this is a serious investment that hotels need to realize is necessary in order to operate properly and efficiently. Gone are the days when we can simply put out a sign and fill our ranks with trained and willing employees. Shame on many of us for not realizing the potential loss and how it could have been averted.

And kudos to those who came up with innovative solutions. I know someone who made sure all their staff was whole—even paid wages for work they didn't do, because they couldn't. Look after your people. It may be time to make some tough decisions, but employees will put up with a lot if they feel you have their back. However, the moment you tell them they're disposable, the relationship was never true to begin with.

Balanced Stewardship. Broadly defined, stewardship is accepting the responsibilities that come with safeguarding the assets of another. In the hotel business, by and large, the managers and brands are promising to do exactly this, with the task being management of the owner's asset. This stewardship relationship became unbalanced when ownership faced heavy losses due to lack of sales during the pandemic. The losses are compounded now because the cost of labor and the furloughing and laying off our team members created a bigger problem: there is no one left to come back. It may sound like I'm playing Monday morning quarterback, but let's call it like it is. When we build up our ranks anew, let's not make that mistake again. Investing in our talent is a requirement for long-term financial health no matter the short-term consequences.

Focus on Profit, Not Just Revenues. For at least a hundred months straight prior to COVID, the hotel industry posted serious gains in REVPAR. Month after month the ceiling was shattered. But what about profits? When the revenue disappears, the profit goes with it. But during the boom we missed the opportunity to maximize the GOPPAR. When I say missed, I mean we didn't measure our profits in a competitive set like we do with REVPAR. The future must include a GOPPAR index with like hotels. This is long overdue.

Check In and Out. After 9/11 we experienced massive changes in how we access our airports and planes. One of the biggest improvements was the kiosks for boarding passes and the last-stop plane boarding scans. Hotels have a massive opportunity to revolutionize check in and out. People do not want to waste time in a line up for a key. Put the technology in the phone and get on with it.

Room Cleaning. The idea that my room needs attending daily was completely thrown out the window in 2020. Let's make sure we don't automatically go back to providing guests with what we think they want. Room attendants are the single biggest labor expense in any hotel. Laundry and amenities are among the two largest expenses. We have before us a golden opportunity to strike a new deal and re-balance the needs of our in-room guest in a post-COVID world. Minimum length-of-stay requirements before automatic cleaning? À la carte cleaning services, perhaps? Give consideration to new approaches that can benefit both hotels and their guests. Don't simply fall back on your old ways of doing things (in my experience this is what happened after the financial crisis of 2008). It's time for thoughtful and innovative leadership.

Improve Technology. Our industry is in need of advancements in technology. The only part of our business that is on any kind of a cutting edge is distribution, and that's almost completely because entities outside of our industry made the investments. With the diverse ownership, branding and franchised landscapes, no one stakeholder wants to take the lead and make the investments that are necessary with technology. It seems like everyone is sitting around waiting for someone else to do the heavy lifting. This is hurting everyone because we don't move forward, and advancements in efficiency will only come through new technology.

My final thought in this chapter is the same as the one that has run through this whole book: Financial Leadership. Having a team of department managers who all know how to manage the middle of their financial statement is what it's all about. Being able to juggle their expenses and payroll when business levels fluctuate is of critical importance to the financial health of the hotel. Without these abilities, leaders will waste resources, and this directly impacts profitability. Now more than ever hotels need a financially engaged team led by the GM and Controller/Director of Finance. Adaptation and flexibility are key, and you need to know your numbers to support this.

Conclusion

I have been writing a weekly blog or publishing a weekly video since 2016. What I have tried to do with this book is tie as many of these thoughts together in a way that will help hoteliers navigate the broad financial landscape of their hotels. I've done this based on my forty years' experience in the field, but even now I'm still learning new things, and I encourage you to do the same: keep learning.

Our business is not terribly complicated, but it is complex. Taken in individual "slices," the various moving parts of a hotel can be relatively uncomplicated, straightforward and easy enough to understand. The complexity comes in because hotels have many departments, most of which are almost always busy.

If we slow down and look at what we're doing—and most importantly who we're being while we're busy with all the doing—we can be more present and deliberate with everything that's happening. Then we'll do a better job and be more effective.

The hotel business for me is a great place to have called home. It's been a pleasure and an honor to share with you my thoughts and experience. I know it's just my take on our industry and how I have seen and experienced it, but I hope it gives you food for thought on your own journey.

Good luck with whatever you're up to and wherever you're at. I will leave you with this reminder of what my dad always said to me:

"Son, you can do anything you want in this world so long as you're willing to work for it."

Other Resources

Mentoring Video

https://qrco.de/bdZ5tC

Asset Management Services Video

https://qrco.de/bdZ5uI

Budget and Proforma Services Video

https://qrco.de/bdZ5vC

Core 5 Workshops Video

https://qrco.de/bdZ5vd

Executive Search Services Video

https://qrco.de/bdZ5vz

Workshops for Financial Leaders

https://qrco.de/bdZ5wS

Hotel Accounting Policy Manuals Videos

https://qrco.de/bdZ5xS

https://qrco.de/bdZ5xz

Workshops for Non-Financial Managers

https://qrco.de/bdZ5z1

Event Speaking Services Video

https://qrco.de/bdZ5zT

Steve Chandler Interview

https://qrco.de/bdZ5zv

Flow-Thru Cheat Sheet

https://qrco.de/bdZ60Y

EFTE & Productivity Exercise

https://qrco.de/bdZ61p

Management Incentive Plan Template

https://qrco.de/bdZ61p

Policy Manual & Internal Control Review Samples

https://qrco.de/bdZ6B1

Bonus Video – How to Turn $250 into $1,000,000 in Asset Value

https://qrco.de/bdZ6DX

Acknowledgments

I would like to acknowledge the following people.

- My lovely wife, Johanne, whose support not only made possible this book but also my business—thank you for never giving up on me and my dream!

- Danny Araujo: his influence and help with my career were incredibly significant.

- Ted Kissane, AKA the Commander: his mentorship and friendship is special and so much of what I know and how it's portrayed in this book is thanks to him.

- Phillipe Borel, AKA the Phantom: tough love, unmatched passion, the best stories, and many valuable lessons learned.

- Ingrid Jarret: your encouragement, and belief in my vision not only fueled me to continue but inspired me as well.

- Maurice Bassett, my publisher: for having the vision and the confidence in the project from the very beginning. Also, for the honest feedback at the start and for sharing those thoughts.

- Jeannie Stinson, my grade four teacher, who reached out after having read one of my blogs, and one thing led to another. She offered to edit the manuscript very early in the process before Maurice agreed to publish. Her dogged edits and honesty made me realize the work that needed to be done and she encouraged me to persevere.

- My editor, Chris Nelson: through the toils of this nearly three-year project his dedication and professionalism never wavered.

- My children: Megan, Alyson, and Sarah, whose love and support I cherish.

- My clients, for your belief in me and your desire to reach for new levels of understanding, performance, and expertise.

- My Mother, Donna: your humor, common sense and love are with me.

About the Author

Davidavid Lund is the award-winning creator of the original Hospitality Financial Leadership workshop, "My Financials," at that time with Fairmont Hotels. He left his day job in 2013 and became The Hotel Financial Coach. He has published a weekly blog to thousands of subscribers since 2016. He has also published over 300 original articles on several hotel industry websites and LinkedIn.

David has held positions as Regional Controller, Corporate Director and Hotel Manager with an international brand for over thirty years. He mentors hospitality leaders, provides online financial workshops, and speaks at hospitality associations and company events. He is the author of the book *The Seven Secrets to Creating a Financially Engaged Leadership Team in Your Hotel* and of a popular online video course. David is a CHAE through HFTP and a Certified Professional Coach.

He is a proud father of three young adults, and is also a grandfather. He and his lovely wife, Johanne, live in Portland, Maine, with their two dogs Max and Dakota. He loves to travel and deliver his workshops throughout North America. You can visit him online at:

www.hotelfinancialcoach.com

MAURICE BASSETT

Publisher's Catalogue

The Mahatma Gandhi Library

#1 Towards Non-Violent Politics

* * *

The Prosperous Series

#1 The Prosperous Coach: Increase Income and Impact for You and Your Clients (Steve Chandler and Rich Litvin)

#2 The Prosperous Hip Hop Producer: My Beat-Making Journey from My Grandma's Patio to a Six-Figure Business (Curtiss King)

#3 The Prosperous Hotelier: A Guide to Hotel Financial Literacy for the Hospitality Professional (David Lund)

* * *

Devon Bandison

Fatherhood Is Leadership: Your Playbook for Success, Self-Leadership, and a Richer Life

Michael Bassoff

RelationShift: Revolutionary Fundraising (Revised Edition) (Steve Chandler and Michael Bassoff)

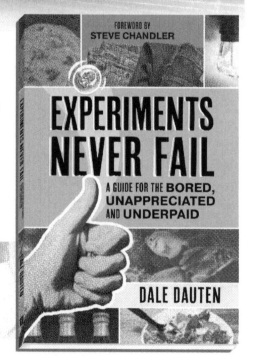

Roy G. Biv

Dancing on Rainbows: A Celebration of Numismatic Art
Early Jack: The "Lost" Photos of John F. Kennedy
Early Jackie: The "Lost" Photos of Jackie Bouvier

Sir Fairfax L. Cartwright

The Mystic Rose from the Garden of the King

Steve Chandler

37 Ways to BOOST Your Coaching Practice: PLUS: the 17 Lies That Hold Coaches Back and the Truth That Sets Them Free
50 Ways to Create Great Relationships
Crazy Good: A Book of CHOICES
CREATOR
Death Wish: The Path through Addiction to a Glorious Life
Fearless: Creating the Courage to Change the Things You Can
How to Get Clients: New Pathways to Coaching Prosperity
The Prosperous Coach: Increase Income and Impact for You and Your Clients (The Prosperous Series #1) (Steve Chandler and Rich Litvin)
RelationShift: Revolutionary Fundraising (Revised Edition) (Steve Chandler and Michael Bassoff)
RIGHT NOW: Mastering the Beauty of the Present Moment
Shift Your Mind Shift The World (Revised Edition)
Time Warrior: How to defeat procrastination, people-pleasing, self-doubt, over-commitment, broken promises and chaos
The Very Best of Steve Chandler
Wealth Creation for Coaches: A Workbook to Create a Prosperous Coaching Practice One Small Step at a Time (Kamin Samuel, PhD and Steve Chandler)
Wealth Warrior: The Personal Prosperity Revolution

George S. Clason

The Richest Man in Babylon

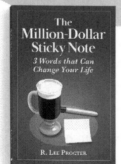

Kazimierz Dąbrowski

Positive Disintegration

Dale Dauten

Experiments Never Fail: A Guide for the Bored, Unappreciated and Underpaid

Charles Dickens

A Christmas Carol: A Special Full-Color, Fully-Illustrated Edition

Anthony Drago

Go Prove Something!

Melissa Ford

Living Service: The Journey of a Prosperous Coach

M. K. Gandhi

Towards Non-Violent Politics (The Mahatma Gandhi Library #1)

James F. Gesualdi

Excellence Beyond Compliance: Enhancing Animal Welfare through the Constructive Use of the Animal Welfare Act

Janice Goldman

Let's Talk About Money: The Girlfriends' Guide to Protecting Her ASSets

Sylvia Hall

This Is Real Life: Love Notes to Wake You Up

Christy Harden

Guided by Your Own Stars: Connect with the Inner Voice and Discover Your Dreams

I ♥ Raw: A How-To Guide for Reconnecting to Yourself and the Earth through Plant-Based Living

Do you struggle to find clients?
To know what to charge?

To balance your professional and social personae?
To truly serve? *Living Service* offers priceless wisdom and
practical tools to help you address these and other essential
questions along the coaching path to prosperity.

"*Living Service* is for coaches
who want better business
results, deeper friendships,
more genuine and loving
family relationships, and
an all-around great life."

~ Sherry Welsh, leadership coach and
author of *Slowing Down: Unexpected
Ways to Thrive as a Female Leader*

Are you ready to turn Pro?

Living Service: The Journey of a Prosperous Coach tells the story of
Melissa Ford's rise from struggling coach to world-class professional.
Raw, honest and full of humor, *Living Service* details Melissa's insecurities
and stumbles along the way, as well as the powerful insights and actions
that transformed her practice—and her life.

Melissa Ford is a master business and life coach with
over twenty years of experience working with clients
individually and in group settings.

Curtiss King

The Prosperous Hip Hop Producer: My Beat-Making Journey from My Grandma's Patio to a Six-Figure Business (The Prosperous Series #2)

David Lindsay

A Blade for Sale: The Adventures of Monsieur de Mailly

Rich Litvin

The Prosperous Coach: Increase Income and Impact for You and Your Clients (The Prosperous Series #1) (Steve Chandler and Rich Litvin)

David Lund

The Prosperous Hotelier: A Guide to Hotel Financial Literacy for the Hospitality Professional (The Prosperous Series #3)

John G. W. Mahanna

The Human Touch: My Friendship and Work with President John F. Kennedy

Abraham H. Maslow

Abraham H. Maslow: A Comprehensive Bibliography
The Aims of Education (audio)
The B-language Workshop (audio)
Being Abraham Maslow (DVD)
The Eupsychian Ethic (audio)
The Farther Reaches of Human Nature (audio)
Maslow and Self-Actualization (DVD)
Maslow on Management (audiobook)
Personality and Growth: A Humanistic Psychologist in the Classroom
Psychology and Religious Awareness (audio)
The Psychology of Science: A Reconnaissance
Self-Actualization (audio)
Weekend with Maslow (audio)

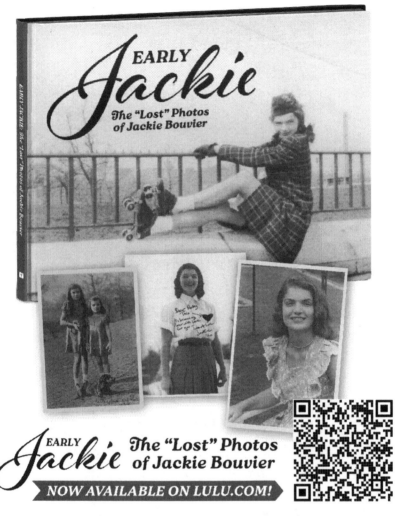

R. Lee Procter

The 50-Minute Coach
The Million-Dollar Sticky Note: 3 Words that Can Change Your Life

Harold E. Robles

Albert Schweitzer: An Adventurer for Humanity

Kamin Samuel, PhD

Wealth Creation for Coaches: A Workbook to Create a Prosperous Coaching Practice One Small Step at a Time (Kamin Samuel, PhD and Steve Chandler)

Albert Schweitzer

Reverence for Life: The Words of Albert Schweitzer

Patrick O. Smith

ACDF: The Informed Patient: My journey undergoing neck fusion surgery

William Tillier

Abraham H. Maslow: A Comprehensive Bibliography
Personality Development through Positive Disintegration: The Work of Kazimierz Dąbrowski

Margery Williams

The Velveteen Rabbit: or How Toys Become Real

www.MauriceBassett.com

Made in the USA
Middletown, DE
15 June 2024

55834064R00175